High Tide

A Practical Guide for Affluent Retirees to Protect, Profit, and Prosper from the Coming Storm

David Boike, DJ Boike, Jake Boike

Disclaimer

This book contains performance data. (Source: Ibbotson Associates and Morningstar.) Presentation of this data is not meant to imply that similar results will occur in the future. Past performance is no indication of future results. Any assertion to the contrary is a federal offense. The data is provided for illustrative and discussion purposes. The performance data cited covers a wide variety of time periods. Rather than focusing on the specific time periods or the results derived, the reader should focus on the underlying principles.

None of the material presented within is intended to serve as the basis for any financial decision, nor does it constitute an offer to buy or sell any security. Such an offer is made by prospectus only, which you should read carefully before deciding to invest any money.

The information presented in this book is accurate and current, to the best of my knowledge. However, performance data changes over time and legislation frequently changes as well. My advice could differ in the future. Therefore, the reader is encouraged to verify the status of such information before investing.

All personal anecdotes are true, but the names have been changed to protect each individual's privacy. It is impossible to ascertain the identity of any person based solely on the information in this book… so if you are a client, friend, or relative of the author, relax!

Table of Contents

Introduction

As an Affluent Retiree, What Can You Do to Protect Your Retirement Dreams?

A perfect storm has arrived for many Americans. The convergence of several key factors threatens the financial security of many people, but especially citizens aged fifty-five and up. For this group of people who are about to retire or have already retired, the threat is very real. According to well-documented sources, most pension funds are underfunded and future benefits may be in jeopardy. The cost of Social Security, Medicaid, and Medicare programs is exploding as more

people retire and fewer taxpayers remain in the workforce. Inflation continues to raise the costs of key goods and services, such as healthcare, alternative housing, utilities, and food. In the meantime, most investors have earned very poor returns on their retirement accounts over the past decade. In addition, taxes are likely to increase again, and guess who will pay the bulk of these tax increases? People who earn over $58,000 per year, which our government considers "rich". In reality, these are simply hardworking people who have saved and invested for their retirement. If this describes you, then brace yourself. You have a great big bull's-eye on your back!

What can you do to protect your retirement dreams?

This book provides answers to that question. After more than thirty years of working in the financial planning industry and meeting thousands of retirees, I have concluded that there are several simple strategies for enjoying a financially safe, secure retirement. Notice that I said several *simple* strategies and not a multitude of *complex* strategies. This is contrary to what most people in the financial industry would have you believe. The complexity lies in knowing what steps to take and what strategies make sense for you. This book will help you find your way.

These are simple common sense strategies that anyone can master and learn to implement. As you read, you will find that this book is really a family affair. It is a compilation of what I have learned in my profession over the past thirty years, as well as the experiences of my two sons, DJ and Jake, who have worked alongside me for the past decade.

In the pages ahead, you will learn the steps we take to help our clients achieve a financially stable, worry-free retirement. As you learn these steps, you will also read testimonials from well-known financial authors and experts.

You will learn about our unique planning process called the ARK program. The ARK program utilizes a step-by-step approach that helps our clients solve their financial problems and achieve their financial goals. The uniqueness of the ARK program is that it was created by us specifically for our clients, rather than a generic program designed by an investment or insurance company to sell their products and services. The ARK program is all about *you* and *your* goals and concerns. As you read, you will see how this unique approach can put you back in control of your retirement.

We sincerely hope that this book will help you avoid the #1 mistake of planning a financially secure retirement: procrastination!

Are you ready to take back your retirement? Are you ready to put the "I can" back into the American Dream? If so, we encourage you to read on, as we share what we have learned from helping many affluent retirees over the past three decades.

An ageless observation:
People don't plan to fail.
They just fail to plan.

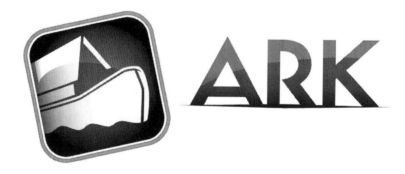

Chapter 1

Step 1:
Reduce Your Investment Fees

How much money are you spending on investment fees?
If you don't know the answer to this question, it's time you find out.
It is essential that you know the cost of every investment you own.
Why? Every dollar you pay in fees is a dollar that stops working for
you. Over time, fees can have a catastrophic effect on your retirement
assets. The more assets you have, the more important it is to know
exactly what you are paying to own and manage them. Affluent
investors are often easy targets for unscrupulous financial advisors
because fees can be easily hidden.

Affluent retirees are easy targets for
unscrupulous financial advisors who cleverly
hide excessive fees within their portfolio.

This chapter will show you how to reduce your investment fees and
keep more of your money.

In this chapter, you will learn:
- The different kinds of investment fees
- How fees can reduce the overall value of your investments
- How to reduce or eliminate some of these fees…and keep
  more of your money!

The Price of Misinformation

Few battles are etched as vividly into our nation's history as the Battle of the Little Big Horn. It isn't the size of the battle that is so intriguing, but the result. General George Custer, one of the battle's major players, is remembered as one of America's most ill-considered and arrogant generals. He has often been criticized for his hasty attack of Sioux Indians encamped along the Little Big Horn River. While it is easy to criticize General Custer for his seemingly impulsive actions, few realize why he made his fatal decision.

General Custer had been sent to southeast Montana to guide the wayward Sioux Indian tribe back to their reservation by the U.S. government. This mission pushed Custer and his men into relatively unfamiliar territory. Upon reaching what was believed to be the only Indian village in the area, Custer sent one Indian scout to determine the number of potential foes. After a couple of hours, the scout returned and *approximated* that there were 800  Indians, mostly women and children. Based on this information, Custer and 277 of his armed men decided to attack. To their surprise, they were met by at least 1,800 Indian warriors specially trained by chiefs Sitting Bull and Crazy Horse. In less than one hour, General Custer and his entire regiment were annihilated. Custer's Last Stand was the disastrous result of misinformation.

You need accurate information about your investments and their fee structures in order to make good decisions. You need to know exactly how your advisor and the investment or insurance company he represents is compensated. You also need to understand the different types of investment fees, including so-called hidden fees.

You may be surprised to learn that many investment fees are as well hidden as the Sioux Indians were to General Custer, and that they can generate additional fees of up to three times more than expected!

What are the different kinds of investment fees?

It is reasonable to pay fees for a service or product, including your investments. Nothing is free. Everything costs money. However, it is unreasonable to be charged *excessive* fees. You need to recognize excessive investment fees.

"How much does it cost to own a mutual fund? Probably a lot more than you think! Trading and transaction costs are very real," says Stephen Horan, head of Professional Education Content and Private Wealth at CFA Institute, a nonprofit association of investment professionals. According to Horan, trading costs for stock funds total about 2–3% of assets annually. You may pay a variety of fees on your investment. Some of the most common are advisory fees, operating expenses, trading costs, administration fees, M&E charges, sales costs, and even marketing fees.

There is a cost for anything of value. Nothing is free. The important issue is that the value of your investment needs to equal or exceed the cost of fees, or you will lose money.

Simply put, fees reduce your assets. The type and amount of investment fees vary by fund and are explained in a fund's prospectus. The total fees charged on common investments, such as mutual funds and variable annuities, can often be 3% or more annually. To understand how a fee affects the value of your investment, here is an example: Suppose that your mutual fund manager earned 6% last year. If the total fees were 3%, your investment nets 3%. You get to keep only half of the gains. Ouch! (Taxes on your gains further reduce the amount of money you get to keep. We will discuss taxes a bit later.)

What happens if your mutual funds lose value over the year? Do your fees get reduced or waived? No. Fees further compound your losses. Think about it like this: if your total fees are 3%, your fund has to earn at least 3% just to break even.

> Funds collect more than $50 billion a year in fees from investors. Near the front of a fund's prospectus, you can see a schedule of fees and expenses, with sales loads listed separately. The numbers may seem harmless…but they can dramatically reduce your returns over time. Despite efforts by the industry to downplay the fee controversy, you should understand this basic fact about funds: **The bite taken out of your investment by fees often determines whether you have gains or losses.**
>
> —Arthur Levitt, former Chairman of the Securities and Exchange Commission

What are hidden fees?

Hidden fees are charges that are not published in the fund prospectus. In a recent *Consumer Reports* article entitled "Don't Get Taken by Hidden Fees", the author estimated that nearly half of the total fees charged on most mutual funds are not disclosed properly, if at all. For example, if an expense ratio is listed as 1–1.5%, there's a good chance that the total fees removed from your account are likely 2–3%.

Don't Get Taken By Hidden Fees!

Another common hidden fee is a turnover or trading cost. You've never heard of a turnover or trading cost? You're not alone. They do not get a lot of publicity in the investment world. They are "incognito" fees that mutual fund companies are not obligated to report.

To understand how these fees work, think of a growth-income mutual fund as a pie chart. One slice of the pie is made up of stock, another slice is made up of bonds, and perhaps another slice consists of cash. Periodically, the fund manager sells some assets to purchase different (hopefully better) assets. Every time he makes a transaction, a fee is charged. It is not uncommon for funds to trade 50–100% of assets in a single year! A manager does not determine the amount of buying or selling he will do throughout the year in advance, so the trading cost does not have to be listed in the prospectus as an expense ratio or fee. It is listed as a fund turnover or trading percentage instead.

"You never have to write a check for trading costs, but the money is seamlessly removed from your total rate of return," explains Don Phillips, Managing Director of Morningstar, a Chicago-based mutual fund research company.

There's a reason you don't consider the costs of investing, of course. Mutual funds and brokers have constructed a system where the costs are practically invisible. You had to write a check to your electric utility or mortgage company, but you've never paid a bill for brokerage or mutual fund management. Such costs are simply deducted from your annual mutual fund returns or taken off the top when a broker executes your trades. You don't notice when 1 percent disappears here, 2 percent there, particularly when your investments are making money. How else can you explain the fact that many Americans react furiously to the $1.50 ATM surcharges they pay, on average, fifty times per year ($75), yet don't utter a peep when they pay a 5 percent sales load on a $10,000 mutual fund investment ($500)?

—Gregory Baer & Gary Gensler, *The Great Trap: How Americans Are Losing Billions to the Mutual Fund and Brokerage Industries—and How You Can Earn More with Less Risk*

How are fees determined?

Let me explain how fees are determined with an analogy. Suppose I walk into Acme Furniture Store and say to the salesperson, "I was at a presentation the other day and they had the most comfortable chairs. I want to get one for myself!" A salesman shows me the chair at a price of $50.00. I say, "Great, I'll pay $50.00 for it." I pay for my chair and take it home. The salesperson makes a full commission and Acme Furniture Company makes a full override because the chair was sold at full price.

Imagine that I go back to the store the following day. I walk in and say, "I love this chair so much that I want to make sure I have one for the rest of my life. I want to buy 100 more." Since I'm buying 100, they offer me a discount. Now I can purchase each chair for $45.00 instead of $50.00. If I buy the chairs at a discount, the store owner and the salesperson lose a little bit of commission and override. They would prefer that I buy the chairs one at a time. That way, they would earn a full override and commission, and they hope to sell the majority of their products at retail price. However, they need to offer wholesale prices in order to be competitive. The same scenario applies to the investment world.

If you walk into ABC Fund Company with $100,000 to invest, will ABC Fund Company take your $100,000? Of course! However, if you walk in with a billion dollars, they will reduce your fees. It's almost like buying in bulk. The larger the investment, the better the pricing. If Warren Buffet has a billion dollars to invest, ABC

Fund Company will offer him lower pricing. This is also true in the brokerage world.

Here's an actual example of how this works. A woman came to our office. She brought a letter that her advisor had sent her (prior to her becoming our client). The letter contained a fee schedule from one of the major brokerage houses in the area. It said that the fee for $2 million or more was 0.5%; for $1 million or more, 0.75%; for $750,000–1 million, 1%; and for $500,000–$750,000, 1.25%. The letter read: " Your account value has dropped below $750,000. You now fall into a new fee schedule category"— which was higher than the previous fee. She said, "Under his management, I've lost $250,000. How can he charge me an extra 0.25%?" Obviously, this woman was very angry and wanted to get her hands around his neck. She certainly wasn't going to pay an extra 0.25% for that kind of service!

This is how the investment world works: the more money you have to invest, the lower your fees. Most people don't have a billion dollars to invest, but consider this: Has your advisor suggested combining your money with a billionaire's so that you can pay lower fees? If your advisor has not teamed you up with a wealthy investor so that you can get institutional pricing rather than retail pricing, you should ask why.

Why hasn't he teamed you up to get institutional pricing? The answer is: He gets paid more to invest your money in retail.

What are the effects of investment fees over time?

Does an extra percent or so make that big a difference? You be the judge. Richard Rutner, author of *The Trouble with Mutual Funds*, describes the effects of fees over time.

"Expense ratios average 1.6% per year, sales charges 0.5%, turnover-generated portfolio transactions cost 0.7%, and opportunity costs [when funds hold cash rather than remain fully invested in stocks] 0.3%. The average mutual fund investor loses 3.1% of his investment returns to these costs each year."

How can you reduce or eliminate some of these fees?
As you can see, fees really do matter! Here are some steps you can take to ensure that you are not paying excessive or hidden fees. Following these simple steps can help you keep more of your money:

1. Get a clear understanding of the investment fees you are paying. Remember the story about Custer? He made a deadly decision based on misinformation. In order for you to make good investment decisions, you need to have good information about the fees you are paying. Start by reading the prospectus. Most clients who come to my office say that they have tried—in vain—to read their prospectus. They get them in the mail month after month. They give a quick look at the cover, see the word *prospectus*, and toss it into the garbage can. I've heard thousands of people say that you have to have a doctorate in finance in order to understand those documents. However, the fee information included in the prospectus is extremely important. If you need help understanding the prospectus, ask a trusted financial advisor to review it for you and explain it to you in layman's terms.

2. Ask a qualified financial advisory firm for a Fee Report. A wise man once said, "If you don't know what you are paying, how do you know if you're getting a good deal?" If your current advisor has not clearly explained exactly what you are paying for your investments, you need to get a Fee Report completed by another qualified financial advisory firm. A properly-prepared Fee Report will detail all of your investment fees and calculate the precise amount that you are paying in fees annually. When I review a Fee Report with a prospective client, they are usually shocked by how much an investment costs them. Though this exercise can be painful, it is necessary if investors want to "heal" their portfolios.

3. Ask about institutional shares. Many of our clients have never been told by their advisor that the same retail mutual fund (A, B, or C shares) can be bought at a lower-priced institutional share. Here's an example from the Morningstar (a third-party research organization that tracks mutual funds) website:

> "Alliance Berstein Global Real Estate Investment B
> and Alliance Berstein Global Real Estate Investment
> I. Investment B has a load of 4%, an expense ratio of
> 2.61%, and a turnover of 0.67%—just over 3% overall.
> Investment I has no load, less than half the expense ratio,
> and a turnover that is exactly the same. Did you know
> that you have the ability to buy either one of the funds I
> just mentioned? By doing so, you can greatly reduce, and
> sometimes eliminate, the amount of fees you're paying for
> your investments."

Some final thoughts about investment fees

It's not what you make, it's what you KEEP that counts! —Proverb

Most people would not purchase a car without knowing the amount of the monthly payment. No one would buy a home without carefully considering the property price and closing costs, and no one would start a home-improvement project without asking the contractor to provide an estimate first.

Shouldn't the same principle apply to your finances?

Most affluent investors did not have their
wealth handed to them on a silver platter.
They worked hard, saved diligently, and
invested faithfully for themselves and
their loved ones.

Let me make a couple of points very clear. First, I am *not* saying that it is wrong for investors to pay a fee to a professional money manager—that would be absurd. Any good or service that an individual purchases has a price. The question is not whether the fee is fair—it's whether the fee is excessive.

Secondly, as an affluent investor, you have the right to know exactly how much you are paying for the services you receive. You have worked hard, saved diligently, and invested faithfully to build your assets for you and your loved ones. If the fees you are being charged reduce the amount of your assets—and they do—then do yourself a huge favor and find a trusted financial professional who utilizes a proven system, such as our ARK program, that helps you detect and diminish the devastating effect that excessive fees have on your retirement assets.

Chapter 2

Step 2:
Minimize Your Tax Obligations

How much are you paying or overpaying on taxes?

This is an important question to answer. Why? Every dollar you pay in taxes is a dollar that stops working for you. Over time, taxes can have a detrimental effect on your retirement assets. This chapter will show you how to pay the taxes you owe, and avoid paying the taxes you don't!

In this chapter, you will learn:

- o How income taxes and estate taxes work
- o How can taxes can decrease the value of your nest egg
- o How you can potentially reduce the amount of taxes on your retirement money.

How to Get Uncle Sam's Attention

In the mid-1920s, notorious gangster Al Capone ruthlessly roamed the streets of Chicago. During that period, Capone and his gang engaged in racketeering, prostitution, gambling, and violence. He was also linked to the St. Valentine's Day Massacre and snubbed his nose at Prohibition. What insidious act finally brought Al Capone to

justice? **Tax evasion**. Racketeering, prostitution, and murder are illegal, but if you *really* want to get Uncle Sam's attention, stop paying your taxes.

Of course, tax evasion is never the answer to paying fewer taxes. You should always seek the counsel of a qualified tax attorney and/ or Certified Public Accountant (CPA) to help you determine the taxes you owe.

Everyone has to either pay taxes or pay the consequences for not doing so. Paying taxes is a necessary price of living in a democratic society. What makes this duty challenging is the fact that the Tax Code frequently changes, and can be difficult to decipher. Sometimes, it is difficult to ascertain the type and amount of taxes that you are legally obligated to pay.

Why do we pay taxes? And why do they keep rising?

Do you think that taxes will rise or change in the near future? Most people would answer a resounding *yes*. The fact is that our country is currently more than $14 trillion in debt and is getting further in debt by the minute. At this point, the U.S. government has no choice but to raise taxes. Here's why: America has a track record of spending far more than it earns. By earning, I am referring to the portion of money the government collects in the form of taxes such as income tax and estate tax. Simply put, what's coming *in* (taxes) is less than what's going *out* (government spending). Rather than reducing spending, many elected officials seem content to pass the buck, meaning huge budget deficits to future generations. It almost seems like a game of fiscal hot potato.

How devastating will the current debt be to the next generation? It's potentially catastrophic. If we eliminate all government spending for the next ten years, every citizen would still be responsible for about $40,000 in tax per year (not including interest).

Why can't the U.S. government just freeze spending or maintain its current spending rates?

Unfortunately, that isn't a solution. Consider this: If the U.S. government required that an additional $2,000 in taxes be paid annually by each of its 309,000,000 citizens, it would take more than 2,000 years to pay back its current debts. Unbelievable? Now consider this: Not everyone is required to pay the same amount of taxes and some do not have to pay any tax at all.

According to the U.S. Census Bureau, nearly seventy-five million citizens are eighteen and under (no taxable income); approximately fifty million are disabled (wages vary due to disability); and thirty million are unemployed. That means 195,000,000 of 309,000,000 U.S. citizens have limited or no taxpaying ability! If you're one of the 114,000,000 U.S. citizens with taxpaying ability, your taxes rise not only to pay your part, but to compensate for those who can't pay.

As our government needs more revenue to meet expanding costs (entitlement programs, debt payments, operating costs, etc.), taxes will rise. If you are an affluent retiree, beware! You are a tax target!

What taxes are you obligated to pay during retirement?

There's no black-and-white answer. Your overall tax obligations depend greatly upon your individual circumstances. This is why consulting a tax attorney and/or CPA is extremely important. However, two types of taxes are an issue for most retirees, so we'll focus on explaining the basics about Income Tax and Estate Tax.

Income Tax

In the United States, a tax is imposed on your income by the federal government, state government, and many local governments. Income tax is determined by applying a tax rate to taxable income as defined by the Tax Code, which may increase as income increases.

Taxable income is your total income less allowable deductions. The word "income" is broadly defined in the Tax Code. Individuals may deduct a personal allowance (exemption) and certain personal expenses, including home mortgage interest, state taxes, contributions to charity, and some other items. Some deductions are subject to limits.

Capital gains are fully taxable and capital losses reduce taxable income only to the extent of gains. Individuals currently pay a lower tax rate on capital gains and certain corporate dividends.

Taxpayers generally must self-assess income tax by filing tax returns. Advance payments of tax are required in the form of withholding tax or estimated tax payments. Taxes are determined separately by each jurisdiction imposing tax. Due dates and other administrative procedures vary by jurisdiction. The due date for filing individual federal, local, and many state returns is April 15th of the following tax year. The amount of tax calculated by the taxpayer may be adjusted by the taxing jurisdiction.

Did you know that Social Security is subject to income tax?

A lot of new retirees are shocked to discover that their Social Security check may be taxable. The usual response is: "You've got to be kidding me! I'm being taxed again?"

There is a common misconception that once you retire, you start paying less in taxes, if any at all, simply because you're no longer working a full-time job and you're in a lower tax bracket. Don't assume, however, that your taxes will be lower in retirement. It's not easy to live on the reduced income needed to qualify for this apparent tax advantage. Furthermore, you'll need to earn more income every year just to keep pace with inflation. So even if you begin your retirement in a lower tax bracket, watch out; you may migrate into a higher one.

—Gregory Salsbury, PhD. *What If I Live? The American Retirement Crisis*, 2006

Estate Tax

Another kind of tax that retirees need to understand is estate tax. According to the IRS, estate tax is a tax on your right to transfer property posthumously. You are required to detail everything you own or have a financial interest in at the time of your death. Furthermore, the fair market value of these items needs to be disclosed—not necessarily what you paid for them or their value at the time you acquired them. The total of all these items is your "Gross Estate". Your property may also include cash and securities, real estate, insurance, trusts, annuities, business interests, and other assets.

Once you have accounted for your Gross Estate, certain deductions (and in special circumstances, reductions in value) are allowed, resulting in your "Taxable Estate". These deductions may include mortgages and other debts, estate administration expenses, and property that passes to surviving spouses or qualified charities. The value of some operating business interests or farms may be reduced for estates that qualify.

After the net amount is computed, the value of lifetime taxable gifts (gifts made from 1977 and onward) is added to this figure and the tax is computed. This tax is further reduced by the available unified credit. Presently, the amount of this credit reduces the computed tax so that only total taxable estates and lifetime gifts that exceed

$1,000,000 actually have to pay tax. In its current form, estate tax only affects the wealthiest 2% of all Americans.

Most relatively simple estates (cash, publicly-traded securities, small amounts of other easily-valued assets, and no special deductions, elections, or jointly-held property) do not require the filing of an estate tax return. Filing is required for estates with combined gross assets and prior taxable gifts exceeding $1,500,000 in 2004–2005; $2,000,000 in 2006–2008; $3,500,000 in 2009; and $5,000,000 or more for 2010 or later. (Note: There are special rules for decedents in 2010.)

How do taxes decrease the value of your nest egg?

Who pays the majority of taxes in America? According to the media, it's not the rich, because they can afford high-priced CPAs to help them take advantage of all of the loopholes. Usually, the top 25% of wage earners pay over 60% of *all* taxes.

How does this affect you? If you make over $58,000 per year, the government considers you "rich". (The U.S. median income is $52,000 per year.)

The vast majority of people we advise have annual incomes of over $58,000. This means that a retired couple with a taxable income of $58,000 per year ($4,833 per month) ends up with a net income of approximately $4,500 per month. Deduct a mortgage payment, utilities, real estate taxes, car payments, food, clothing, and healthcare expenses, and that $4,500 is gone. Yet the government still considers you "rich".

Many of our new clients ask, "Why did we have to pay Social Security taxes all those years we worked? Now that we are retired and receiving benefits, we have to pay taxes again? That doesn't seem fair." In my opinion, they are right. It isn't fair! However, the government needs the money and they are going to take it wherever they can.

It is not just your pension, Social Security, dividends, and interest that the government targets. They are also eyeing your IRAs (individual retirement accounts), 401ks, and inheritances.

How can you reduce tax on your retirement assets?

Every retiree who has worked hard and saved money has to deal with taxes. Unless you are willing to "keep giving till it hurts", you need to make tax planning an important part of your financial plan.

Where you focus your investments and where you derive your income in retirement affects the amount you pay in taxes. The days of simply chasing the highest returns without regard for how you will convert that investment income are over.

> As this greatest transfer of wealth in human history reaches its apex in the coming years, there will be an explosion of excessive taxation that will reach epidemic proportions (especially given the population affected), an explosion that will give millions of ill-prepared and under-protected American savers like yourself the financial shock of their lives. The fallout from this "retirement savings time bomb" will continue to affect you, your children, the economy, and society for years and years to come.
>
> —Ed Slott, CPA. *The Retirement Tax Bomb and How to Defuse It*, 2008.

Some final thoughts about taxes

Many people have the misconception that once you retire, you start paying less in taxes because you're not working full-time and you're in a lower tax bracket. Don't assume that your taxes will be lower in retirement. It's not easy to live on the reduced income needed to qualify for this apparent tax advantage. Furthermore, you'll need to earn more income every year just to keep pace with inflation. Even if you begin your retirement in a lower tax bracket, watch out. You may migrate to a higher one.

Taxes will become an even bigger concern for affluent retirees in the future.

Tax planning will become increasingly important to affluent retirees as our government desperately tries to raise revenue for the growing costs of Social Security, Medicare, and Medicaid programs. Add our nearly 15-trillion-dollar debt and you'll see where the economy is heading. People with money will be targeted. If that describes you, you may be a candidate for our ARK program.

Chapter 3

Step 3: Protect Your Nest Egg

How will a market downturn affect your nest egg?

As you near retirement or begin life as a retiree, your retirement accounts may not have enough time to make up for those losses, especially if a downturn is significant (such as the market drop that occurred in 2007–2008). As a result of that downturn, Americans lost $2.8 trillion or 32% of their market-linked investments. This chapter explains the effects of market risks and how you can combat them.

In this chapter, you will learn:

o   How market risks threaten your retirement income as you near retirement or officially retire

o   What the Rule of 100 can tell you (or not tell you) about risk

o   How to protect your nest egg.

Risking It All to Acquire More

The Roman Empire was long considered one of the greatest empires of all time. At its peak, it had unrivaled power. No one dared to challenge the infamous Roman army and risk its wrath. At the pinnacle of its existence, Rome extended as far north as England, as far west as the Atlantic, as far east as Turkey, and as far south as the northernmost tip of Africa. Despite its power, Rome had one distinct flaw: manufacturing. Rome had no major manufacturing base and was forced to reach outside its Italian borders to acquire wealth. Essentially, Rome extracted 100% of its wealth by attacking towns and villages, pillaging, and plundering. With each conquest, the Romans migrated farther from Italy to obtain wealth. The further they traveled to acquire wealth, the longer the Roman soldiers left the Empire unprotected and its acquisitions vulnerable.

As time passed, villagers and a group of barbarians known as the Visigoths began to notice the Romans' propensity for long absences. They took advantage of their absence as an opportunity to regain their wealth. They mobilized armies and waited for the Romans to march off to their next destination. As soon as the Romans were out  of sight, the Visigoths attacked Rome. In less than a week, Rome was completely overtaken. Rome fought to retain the city, but the damage was done. It was never able to regain its former strength.

How market risks can deplete your nest egg

Rome extended itself well beyond its safety zone in order to acquire more than it had already accumulated. Many investors do the same—they risk the assets they've worked so hard to accumulate in order to acquire more wealth. This can expose your nest egg to irreplaceable losses.

Have you ever heard this advice? *Don't worry about the risk. Just hang on to your investments and in time you will be rewarded.* Or how about this? *Stock market investors always earn 10–12% over time.* It sounds easy enough: just go online, buy some stock, and start raking in the growth! Unfortunately, it's not that simple.

Every day, we meet a client who has bought into the myth that the best strategy to financial security in retirement is simply investing all or most of your funds in the stock market. *Don't worry about the risk of loss, fees, or running out of money. Follow my great stock-picking strategy and you will be rich!* Yet when we listen to our new clients' statements and do some research, the reality is very different than the story they have been sold.

In the article "How to Lose $9 Trillion in a Bull Market", Jason Zweig highlighted a study which explained that average stock market returns are much lower than commonly reported. According to the thirty-year study he cited (from 1973–2003), the stock market rose 9.6% per year—yet the average investor only received 4.3%. This return is not much better than what they would have received from low-risk CDs and other fixed rate accounts. Let's examine this again: over 25 years, the NASDAQ Index rose 9.6%, but investors only earned 4.3%. What happened to the other 5.3%? When we tell people that the interest was likely lost to excessive fees and poor advice, they are often shocked. They say: *The market went up over 9% and I only got to keep 4%? That's not fair!* They have every right to be upset.

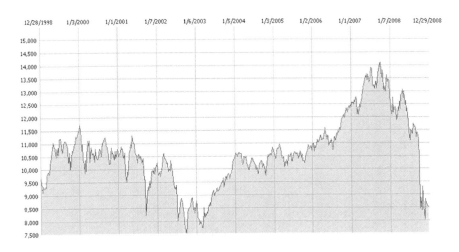

Recently, many investors who fully invested in the stock market from 1999 to 2009 saw little or no gain in their portfolios. The story was even more bleak for retired investors who received monthly income checks from their IRAs. Depending on how much of their money was invested, many of those retirees have significantly fewer retirement assets than they did five or ten years ago. This past decade revealed a costly reality: buying and holding stock does not always guarantee that you will make money.

Consider this: the Dow Jones Index closed on December 31, 1999 at about 11,497. Ten years later, on December 31, 2009, the Dow Jones closed at 10,428. Over ten years, there was no gain. That's why 2000–2009 has become known as the "lost decade" for many investors. (In 2011, at the time of writing this book, the Dow Jones Index continues to fluctuate between 11,000 and 12,500, still down substantially from its high of 14,164 in October 2007.)

> *The old saying "It's not what you make, it's what you keep" is never more important than during retirement.*

As we reach retirement, avoiding risk becomes as important as accumulating interest. What took thirty years to accumulate can be reduced significantly in as little as one year. If you have $1 million saved for retirement, how much would your life change if you earned 10% interest ($100,000)? The gain is nice, but it probably isn't enough to significantly alter your lifestyle. However, what if you lost 30%-40% ($300,000-$400,000) of those retirement dollars? Do you think your lifestyle would change?

People are beginning to question the advice they have been hearing for years. *Does it really make sense to have the majority of my retirement funds invested in stocks? Is the risk really worth it? Does "buy and hold" still work? Is there a better way to harness the power of the stock market and reduce the chances of losing accumulated assets of thirty or forty years?* These are the kinds of questions we hear every day. Fortunately, there are answers!

The sage advice "Buy & Hold" should be
renamed "Buy & Hope"

What can the "Rule of 100" tell you about market risks?

The Rule of 100 is a rule of thumb that can help you determine how much money you should allocate to your retirement and investment accounts, how much of that money should be at risk in the stock market, and how much should be in "safe" places. To use the Rule of 100, take the number 100 and subtract your age. The remainder will tell you approximately what percentage of your retirement assets should be invested in risky ventures like equities and stocks, and what percentage of your assets should be allocated to safe investments.

To understand how this works, here's an example. Let's say you are thirty years old, employed, and contributing weekly to your 401k or 403b account. Using the Rule of 100, a thirty-year-old individual should allocate about 70% of his or her portfolio into more risk-based options that are focused on growth. The other 30% should be invested more conservatively. When the market goes down, your contribution buys more shares. If the market moves up—and historically it has—you make more money. Market declines can actually be an opportunity for investors who don't plan to use their assets for years.

Conversely, if you are a seventy-year-old retiree who is not contributing to retirement accounts, market declines are not an opportunity. On the contrary, they are a foe. If the stock market drops 30–40% and a retired investor has most of his money in the stock market, he will lose that 30–40%. Since the retiree is not contributing any new money, there is little opportunity to capitalize on market activity.

Properly implemented, the Rule of 100 can protect a retiree's portfolio. Based on the Rule of 100, a seventy-year-old should have 70% or more of his retirement assets in safe options, such as conservatively-managed bond funds, CDs, and fixed annuities. If the stock market loses half of its value, these types of accounts will help protect your nest egg. The other 30% can still be invested in the stock market. However, in order to reduce risk and fees, we do not recommend that you use retail mutual funds (which most brokers sell), and we advise against doing this yourself. Seek the counsel of a trusted advisor who gets compensated to advise you as opposed to selling to you. Be sure to read chapter Seven, where we discuss how the right advisor can save you thousands of dollars.

What can you do to combat market risks?

On average, Americans work thirty to forty years to grow a nest egg that will secure their retirement years for them and their loved ones. Unfortunately, too many retirees act on advice from well-meaning friends, family, and financial advisors (and some not-so-well-meaning advisors) that may prove disastrous! Here is a real-life example.

A woman came to my office. She and her husband were business owners and had saved their entire lives. Her husband was the primary businessperson in the family. She didn't look at the financial statements or examine the books of the business. He ran the business and the finances. It seems old-fashioned now, but there was a time when women didn't have much say in the finances of the home. However, it is now 2011, and it is essential for women to be involved in the finances of their own homes, and work with their husbands on building for their retirement. This woman didn't. She grew up in an era in which it was customary to leave the finances to her husband.

Eventually, the husband retired and sold the business for over $1 million. Since he was a business owner, he had no pension—but he did have Social Security and a pretty nice nest egg. His plan was to draw 3% per year from their retirement assets and live on $50,000 per year for the rest of their lives. Two years after he sold the business, the husband died. His wife—who had no dealings with the money at any point in her life—was now money manager for the estate. (If you're a woman, the chance of you becoming the money manager of a retirement plan or estate is quite high. Women generally outlive men by up to seven years. Furthermore, men usually marry younger women, so those numbers are even more inclined toward the woman.)

The wife was now in charge of a $1.2 million portfolio. She had never looked at a statement in her life and she didn't start when her husband passed away. Financial statements began to pile up on her desk because she didn't understand them. Yet she continued to withdraw money from the accounts. The value of the portfolio dropped rapidly. She was frightened because the accounts kept decreasing. Eventually, she just stopped opening the financial statements. One day, her daughter came for a visit and noticed the unopened mail. She asked her mother about it and her mother said, "Those are just my financial statements." Her daughter replied, "Mom, shouldn't you be looking at your statements each quarter? What if your accounts are going down?" The woman told her daughter that she didn't understand the statements, so what was the point?

Finally, the daughter asked her mother if she could look at the statements. The woman told her that since the money would be hers someday, feel free to open the envelopes. As the daughter examined the latest statement, she was shocked.

The panicked daughter brought her mother to our office with the statement she had read. After perusing it, I asked the woman if she had been withdrawing only 3% from her account. She said that this was true. She thought she was taking only $36,000 out of her $1.2 million account per year, which should have been extremely easy to do, even at fixed rates. What she didn't know is that her account was dropping until it finally decreased to half of the prior amount in October 2008. The account was now worth only half of its original amount. Instead of taking 3% of $1.2 million to get $36,000 per year, she had been taking closer to 5% of $700,000 to get her desired $36,000 per year. The market was not going up at that time. The woman was taking a higher percentage of income than she realized and the account was decreasing. At this point, her concern became running out of money. Her case was heartbreaking because I couldn't go back and erase the last six years of transactions. I could only work with the remainder of the account.

Why would an advisor put a retired widow in a position where she had lost half of her money?

What can you do to protect your nest egg?

To protect yourself from the risk of losing principal when you can least afford it, you need to think and act differently. Here are some things you can do to protect your nest egg from market-related risks:

1. Think differently. Incorporate new thinking into your retirement planning. The younger you are, the more time you have to make up for losses and mistakes. The older you are, the effects of losses and mistakes increase the risk of damage to your financial security. Using the Rule of 100 as a starting point, you need to determine the combination of "risk money" options and "safe money" options that are right for you.

2. Consider safe money options. Plan now to manage risk and avoid large losses. In other words, assess the amount of your risk money and safe money investments. While you are assessing them, you may want to recalculate the amount of money you invest in each option, as shown in the chart below:

Retirement Assets	Options	Pros	Cons
Risk Money	o Mutual funds o Commodities o Real estate o Stocks o Bonds o Money market accounts	o Growth potential o Investment options	o Penalties for early withdrawals o Potential to lose some or all of your principal
Safe Money	o Savings accounts o Savings bonds o Certificates of deposit o Fixed annuities	o Principal protection o Guaranteed interest	o Charges and penalties for early withdrawals o Occasional lower interest rates

This chart is only a guide to give you a general idea about Risk Money Options and Safe Money Options, which you can allocate to your retirement assets. A trusted financial advisor can help you determine how much of your retirement assets you should reposition from Risk Money Options to Safe Money Options.

3. Get professional financial advice. The average American works thirty to forty years to build a nest egg that will help them and their loved ones enjoy their retirement. Unfortunately, too many retirees act on advice given by well-meaning friends, family, and financial advisors, which may actually prove disastrous. Seek the support of a trusted financial advisor who has the training and experience to help you make good financial decisions.

Some final thoughts about market risks

Americans plan and live in retirement differently now. Past generations relied heavily on the government for Social Security and on employers' pensions to provide them with guaranteed retirement income.

Now we are not only responsible for saving enough money *before* we retire; we're also responsible for planning how we'll convert that money into income *after* we retire. Along with this responsibility comes risk—such as market risks.

> *High risk does not always equal high returns.*
> *If it did, everyone would come home rich*
> *from Las Vegas!*

Fortunately, there are solutions that can help you **minimize** your retirement risks and **maximize** your retirement assets. A trusted financial advisor can help you:

- o **Identify** how market risks can affect your nest egg
- o **Gain** helpful ideas for addressing these risks
- o **Allocate** your retirement dollars in the right way for you.

A comprehensive review of your current investment portfolio along with an unbiased discussion of all options available can be of great help to you. Find a trusted financial advisor who uses a diagnostic approach (such as our ARK program) to effectively help you preserve your retirement nest egg for you and your loved ones.

Chapter 4

Step 4:
Maximize Your Returns

How can you maximize the returns on your retirement assets?

Maximizing your returns is a relative phrase. What it means is doing the best with what you have or taking advantage of opportunity. Who's to say what percentage of gain is the best maximization of your portfolio? A 0% return in the market meltdown of 2008 was considered a success by most financiers. Any investor should take advantage of the opportunities afforded to him every year. We don't know when an opportunity will arise, but we must be prepared to take action when it does.

In this chapter, you will learn:
  o   How to recognize a few so-called "strategies" that rarely work
  o   How to execute a simple strategy that does work
  o   How to minimize your risks and maximize your returns.

The primary objective of an intelligent investment strategy should be to *preserve capital* and build on it at a consistent, moderate rate in both bull and bear markets.

—Edward Winslow, *Blind Faith: Our Misplaced Trust in the Stock Market and Smarter, Safer Ways to Invest*

Tom Brady and His Captured Opportunity

The National Football League (NFL) is enormously competitive. On average, an NFL career lasts three years or less, but some players would give anything to have that limited opportunity. Even if a player is selected during the draft—the lower the pick, the lower the chance that the player will make it onto a team.

In 2000, a quarterback named Tom Brady broke the mold. He was drafted in the seventh round, 199th overall. Six other quarterbacks were chosen ahead of Brady. Four are no longer in the league and two have achieved nowhere near his success.

During his inaugural professional football season, Brady languished on the New England Patriots bench waiting for his opportunity behind the #1 overall pick in the 1993 NFL Draft, Drew Bledsoe. Brady worked with his advisors and prepared himself, waiting for his opportunity. In the second game of Brady's second season, Bledsoe was injured and Brady became the starter. He stepped in and took advantage of his opportunity by leading the Patriots to the Super Bowl title. This was only the first of his Super Bowl titles! Brady is now  widely regarded as one of the best professional quarterbacks of all time, as well as one of the richest. How did he accomplish this? The answer is that he was ready to take advantage of the opportunity when it presented itself.

Capturing your opportunities

You must be prepared to seize opportunities to maximize your investments. First and foremost, it is crucial that you find a professional money manager to research the profitability and solvency of company stocks and bonds. These money managers are similar to

Tom Brady taking the opportunity to maximize his potential. You need to assemble a team of quality advisors and money managers who specialize in seeking out these opportunities. The average individual has neither the time nor the knowledge to do this. Maximize your returns by maximizing your research and advisory staff.

When it comes down to it, monthly income determines the lifestyle most retirees live. After thirty years of working with retirees, I am convinced that most retirees are more concerned about the amount of income they receive each month rather than what they grow in their investment accounts.

Remember when the ideal retirement consisted of having a good pension, Social Security, no debts, and enough cash in the bank to help you enjoy your golden years? Things have changed. Pension checks have either been reduced or are in jeopardy. Social Security is no longer guaranteed to increase annually or even to exist in the future. Debt of all kinds—especially mortgages and credit card debt—are obligations in many retirees' monthly expenses. What about bank accounts? A lot of money is still in banks, but it is only earning a tiny fraction of the interest it used to earn. Remember when a CD paid 5%, 10%, or even 12%? A $100,000 CD at 12% provided an estimated $1,000 in retirement income each month with little or no risk. It used to be a no-brainer purchasing CDs! Now those same banks that were paying 5–12% are paying approximately 1% or less. The $1,000 monthly check you used to receive years ago (or used to compound in your account) is now worth only about $100 each month. Times certainly have changed!

Today's retirees need to be just as concerned about providing themselves with additional monthly income for the rest of their lives as they are about the amount of their nest egg. As one new client said recently, "I can't spend what's on that statement. I can only spend what comes to me each month."

The fastest way to make the highest return on your investments is to put it all in the stock market. You may hear things like: *Don't worry about the risk, just get in the game and stay there. Hire a professional stock picker (stockbroker) and let him move your money around between stocks and stock mutual funds. Better yet, do it yourself and save big money! It's so simple. Everybody makes money investing in the stock market.*

This kind of financial advice is not useful. In fact, it's about as sensible as someone telling you to gamble your assets in Las Vegas.

"Just as a fortunate few will walk away winners while the majority of the players lose, the rules of this game favor the house," Edward Winslow, author of *Blind Faith*, explains. "The people at the top rake in obscene truckloads of money in frenzied rising markets, and even make carloads when the market is going down. Investors have every right to feel taken advantage of."

Your strategy for maximizing returns on your investments should not mimic those of a Las Vegas casino. Rather, pre-retirees and retirement investors need a proven strategy to maximize their returns while minimizing their risks. You must not gamble with your investments. The cost of losing is too high.

Strategies that do not work

Before I show you how we help our clients maximize their returns while minimizing their risks, take a look at a few common mistakes.

Mistake 1: Get your advice from your favorite TV, radio, or financial publications

As John Merrill, author of *Outperforming the Market,* points out, investors need to be aware of the bias of the financial press. They must remember that the job of the media is to maintain and increase their audience. They do so by getting listeners and readers hooked on the "daily drug" of financial information. In order to be successful, the media must convince investors that all of their information is valuable and isn't just noise. Radio, TV, and magazines make money by selling advertisements. Is some of their information helpful? Of course! Always keep in mind, however, that their main goal is to appeal to as wide an audience as possible, so that they can earn maximum advertising revenue.

Mistake 2: Chase last year's winners

Some people believe that assembling a winning portfolio of mutual funds is as simple as picking up the latest copy of *Money* magazine and selecting last year's winners. Unfortunately, history shows us that this strategy rarely works. Last year's winners are most often this year's losers.

> "The biggest investment mistake people make is focusing on last year's mutual fund performance and not on what really drives returns."
>
> —Barbara Raasch, partner at Ernst and Young. *Business Week*, February 22, 1999.

However, although chasing last year's top performers rarely results in a winning strategy, it does sell a lot of magazines!

Mistake 3: Rely on research from the brokerage industry

We always need to put serious thought into major decisions. We have all heard the phrases "Do your homework" or "Do some research". Better yet (we have also been told), save your time and let our financial advisor (broker) do the work. After all, his or her parent company has one of the largest research departments in the country. However, when is research not really research?

As investors, we have discovered that much of the research and advice distributed by the brokerage industry was totally self-serving and worse than worthless. Those who followed the advice of the large brokerage institutions during the collapse of the market bubble in early 2000 suffered big-time losses as analysts privately called the same stocks they were recommending pieces of junk.

—Edward Winslow, *Blind Faith.*

Too much of what is believed to be research has turned out to be nothing more than a sales pitch that benefited the broker and his company.

The interview I remember most vividly is the one that I had with Merrill Lynch. This was the firm that I was exposed to many years earlier and in my mind was the biggest, the most prestigious, and the best. Boy was I in for a shock! In the interview I emphasized my knowledge and experience of accounting, financial analysis, and economics. The interviewer told me, "All that crap won't do you any good here. We're looking for salesmen. We tell you what to sell and train you in how to sell it. We're looking for people with a basic background in sales whom we can mold into productive stockbrokers. Brokers are salespeople, period. We have other people in the firm that analyze stuff."

—Edward Winslow, *Blind Faith.*

You will learn how to find a trusted advisor who is *not* a salesperson, but someone who truly represents you, as you read on.

Mistake 4: Believe that "buy and hold" works for every investor

This strategy works on the premise that in order to outperform all other investment strategies, all you need to do is buy stock and hold it long-term. It is "time in the market, not market timing" that will make you a successful investor.

The bear market of 2000–2002 epitomized the folly of this strategy. Retired investors who could not afford to lose their money watched helplessly as their investment accounts declined dramatically.

They followed the advice of their advisors and held onto their funds staunchly, then watched helplessly as they quickly lost money—in some cases, a great deal of money.

Can a "buy and hold" strategy work? Yes, it can—if you wait a substantial period of time. How long is long enough? Nobody knows for sure. There has been only one profitable twenty-year holding period: 1929–1949.

Fast forward to today: The NASDAQ, from 2000 to 2002, suffered a greater percentage loss than the stock market in 1929. How long will it take to come back? Is it possible that we could be facing another twenty-year holding period? It's possible, but no one knows for sure. If you are retired, can you afford to wait twenty years for your portfolio to recover?

Mistake 5: Believe that mutual funds are the best tool for long-term investors

Mutual funds are marketed as being the best investment tool for long-term investors. Are they?

In 2002, a record 373 funds were liquidated and shut down. Another 733 funds were merged into other funds. Why were so many funds closed? Many funds are created to capitalize on investing trends. If a trend has run its course, the fund gets closed. Also, many funds get closed simply due to poor performance. (This will be discussed later in this book.)

While financial advisors and the mutual fund industry have preached the buy and hold strategy of investing, mutual fund managers appear not to subscribe to that theory. The average mutual fund has a turnover rate of 110%. This means that the entire portfolio is sold slightly more than once a year. In truth, mutual fund managers are short-term speculators, not long-term investors. Yet mutual fund managers push the investor to buy and hold for the long-term.

> In the greatest of all bull markets, funds of all sizes seriously underperformed the stock market. The inability of 85% of all fund managers even to match the performance of the market overall is the result of high fees, operating costs, short-term investment horizons, and substantial transaction and tax costs.

> —Richard Rutner, *The Trouble with Mutual Funds*

A simple strategy that works

Now that you know that some strategies are actually mistakes, let me tell you about a strategy that works. Remember the Rule of 100? Well, the Rule of 100 can also help maximize your returns while minimizing your risks. Here's a secret you rarely hear from most financial advisors: If you don't suffer big losses on a large portion of your retirement assets, lower returning assets can increase your overall return. In other words, it isn't always wisest to go for the highest possible returns. It can be more important to avoid the huge losses that tend to occur in the stock market every five or six years.

Here is an example of how the Rule of 100 may help a seventy-year-old retired investor maximize his returns while minimizing his risks:

Step 1. Allocate 70% of his retirement accounts into safer options designed to protect his principal and provide a source of predictable income.

Step 2. Allocate the remaining 30% of his retirement accounts into an institutionally-managed separate account to reduce fees, while providing a higher level of management. (Notice I did not say a portfolio of mutual funds.)

Why do I recommend that affluent investors use institutionally-managed separate accounts rather than the traditional retail mutual funds offered by brokers? It comes down to fees and performance. In my professional experience, separate accounts are much smarter for older investors with significant assets.

By allocating his retirement accounts based on the Rule of 100, a seventy-year-old investor can accomplish the basic goals of preserving his account value while having the opportunity to maximize his returns.

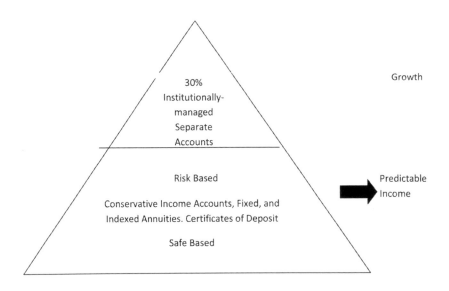

What are separate accounts?

Separate accounts are portfolios of individual securities that are managed independently by an institutional investment manager on your behalf. A manager purchases a customized selection of securities for your portfolio, in accordance with your investment objectives. These securities are registered in your name and traded on your behalf. Based on your input, your advisor will select the most appropriate investment strategy to help meet your needs, and then choose the institutional investment manager who will help you achieve your objectives. You may have more than one institutional investment manager, choosing specialists in different styles or sectors.

How do separate accounts compare to mutual funds?

Separate accounts are similar to mutual funds in that they offer the benefits of professional money management and diversification. Unlike mutual funds, however, separate accounts provide the following additional features:

- o Access to institutional investment managers
- o A broad selection of institutional investment managers with whom you might not usually do direct business
- o Portfolio customization and control
- o The ability to tailor a portfolio to suit your particular needs, such as choosing not to invest in certain types of companies or market sectors
- o The ability for you and your advisor to decide which securities should be liquidated, as well as the timing of those sales

More effective tax management

Individual securities that comprise your portfolio are purchased at the time you open your account, and a cost basis is established at the time of purchase. Your institutional investment manager uses this information to control the amount and timing of the realization of capital gains and losses. This may help you manage the overall tax impact of securities transactions on your financial situation more effectively.

Controlling distribution of realized capital gains and losses

Only realized capital gains are distributed with mutual funds, which creates taxable income. In a separate account, realized losses may help to offset your tax liabilities. This is a benefit if you realize a taxable income or taxable capital gains outside of your managed investment portfolio.

Separate accounts allow you to access a high level of investment management not typically available to retail mutual fund investors. Amazingly, most of our clients pay *fewer* fees to have their money in institutionally-managed separate accounts rather than pay their registered representative (broker) to recommend mutual funds.

> Originally introduced in late 1996, assets in separately
> managed accounts have grown at an average annual rate of 30%
> according to the Money Management Institute. At the end
> of 2003, assets held in these types of accounts industry-wide
> topped the half-trillion-dollar mark for the first time, ending
> the year at $508 billion. Industry researchers predict total assets
> to grow to nearly $2.2 trillion by 2011.
>
> —*The Money Management Institute Press*, April 1, 2004

Some final thoughts about maximizing returns while minimizing risks

Protected investments safeguard your principal while providing a return that is tied to the market. Protected investments include: market-linked certificates of deposit, market-linked notes, fixed index annuities, and equity-linked life insurance. Your principal is guaranteed and/or insured by major financial institutions that are able to provide these assurances. Your risk of loss is effectively transferred to a third party.

Edward Winslow, author of *Blind Faith*, summed up this philosophy by writing, "The primary objective of an intelligent investment strategy should be to preserve capital and build upon it at a consistent, moderate rate in both bull and bear markets. Our personal definition of risk is simple and understandable: we don't want to lose money. But many of us are shooting at the wrong target."

If you want to safely maximize the returns on your retirement funds, find a trusted financial professional who can show you how to correlate growth and guaranteed types of accounts within your portfolio. A strategy like our ARK program is designed to do that.

Chapter 5

Step 5:
Establish a Supplemental
Guaranteed Income Strategy

Income has emerged as a top priority for most retirees. In nearly every survey of pre-retirees and retired investors, the foremost concern that most people have is running out of income in their retirement years. The strategy above deals with the primary concern of losing income.

> *According to numerous surveys, the #1 financial concern among affluent retirees is not having enough income to finance their retirement.*

Why are so many people concerned about having enough income to last throughout their retirement? Remember the days when you worked thirty years at a company and retired with a good pension, full healthcare benefits, and Social Security? You had the ability to retire and take vacations, buy a new car every few years, purchase a second home or condo in a

warm-weather state, help your grandchildren save for college, and/or donate to an institution that you care about (church or charities). Remember those retirement dreams?

Times have definitely changed! Many retirees who once dreamed of helping others are now justifiably concerned about helping themselves.

In this chapter, you will learn:

- o Why income has become a top priority for today's retirees
- o How retirement planning can give you a reliable source of income for life
- o How to create a backup plan or "Plan B" in case of emergency.

Join the Club

The population in need of retirement planning is growing. In 2020, 100 million Americans will be aged fifty-five and up, according to the U.S. Census. Yet many of them will be ill-equipped to live in retirement. The more under-prepared you are for retirement, the more dependent you will become on pensions and Social Security. As more retirees draw on their pensions and Social Security, the more programs will be depleted.

Let's discuss Social Security. The Social Security Administration estimates that it will soon receive 16,000 new benefit applications daily. Social Security is on the verge of bankruptcy. There are simply too many people drawing from a resource that is funded by a declining number of workers. Many reports forecast that unless we make some major changes now, the Social Security Administration will be bankrupt in just a few years. Meanwhile, our elected officials continue to pass this political hot potato back and forth because nobody wants to cut a grandmother's Social Security check.

At least you can count on your pension, right? Unfortunately, both private and public pensions are drastically underfunded. To make matters worse, the Pension Benefit Guarantee Corporation (PBGC), which is responsible for insuring pensions, is also severely underfunded.

The future stability of pensions and Social Security benefits is out of our control, so we must focus our attention on a situation in which we do have control: our personal retirement assets.

Proper retirement planning focuses not only on the first few years of retirement, but on long-term security, or how to reliably generate income for twenty-five years or more.

The proper focus of retirement planning is less about finding the "best" stock to buy and more about creating long-term retirement security.. *If sufficient income is the #1 concern and objective of competent retirement planners, why are so many financial advisors trying to sell you the latest stock or mutual fund of the week?*

According to a recent study by T. Rowe Price, an investor started with a $500,000 portfolio on January 1, 2000, and invested 55% in stocks, 45% in bonds, and withdrew the recommended 4% per year. This investor now has a 71% chance of running out of money during retirement. *But you were told not to worry about risk...buy and hold... Just hang on!* Isn't it wise to consider all your options before this happens to you?

"Buy and Hold" has become "Buy and Hope"!

How much income can you afford to withdraw from your nest egg when you retire?

It was easy to be optimistic about retirement income in the late 1990s. Many investors' portfolios just seemed to go up and up. Buoyed by their swollen investments, many investors were convinced that they could sustain withdrawal rates of 7% or more each year—*and* count on rising stocks prices to maintain the value of their portfolios and even increase them! Americans were in love with the market. Then the bubble burst. The worst bear market (2000–2002) since the Great Depression brought investors back to reality. Many retirees began reducing their budgets, changing their lifestyles, and even returning to the workforce to cope with their newfound financial shortfalls.

Creating additional sources of reliable retirement income

Every retiree will probably need additional income during retirement. How can you create it? If you read *Money* magazine and others like it, it may seem like there are hundreds of ways to make a fortune. However, the truth is that there are only a few options that reliably provide the high level of guarantees, safety, growth potential, and income that retirees need. Before explaining these options, consider common strategies that <u>do not</u> work well for generating safe, stable, and predictable income for retirees.

1. Systematic withdrawals from brokerage accounts or mutual fund portfolios. Have you ever been told that you could safely withdraw 8% from your accounts because the stock market averages more than 10% per year? Suddenly, financial experts lowered that withdrawal percentage to 6%, then 5%, and most recently, 4%. Recent studies advise you not to withdraw more than 3% from your portfolio each year. Why? A bad year or two can really devastate a retiree's portfolio and significantly reduce the amount of income you can withdraw each month <u>without</u> worrying about emptying your accounts.

> *When you draw income from a mutual fund portfolio that you purchased when shares were higher, you have to sell more shares to create desired income. We call this disastrous strategy "Reverse Dollar Cost Averaging".*

2. Taking interest off CDs, savings accounts, and/or money market accounts. Remember when you could get 12% on a CD from your local bank? It was so simple! 12% on a $100,000 CD paid $12,000 in interest each year. At 12%, you received $1,000 per month guaranteed, with no risk to your principal. It was a retiree's dream! Unfortunately, times have changed. Now that same $100,000 CD only pays 1–2%, which generates about $80–160 interest per month.

> *Your money may be "safe" at the bank, but this just means that you are going backward safely.*

3. Taking dividends from stocks. In the past, an individual could simply diversify among a variety of successful company stocks and live off the dividend checks like clockwork—until some big companies, including financial institutions, went bankrupt. Now many stock certificates are not even worth the paper they're printed on. Needless to say, these three common strategies no longer work the way they used to. The more volatility in the stock market and with interest rates, the more important it is to find a safer way to generate the additional monthly income a retiree needs.

A Step-by-Step Approach to Retirement Income Planning

Now that you've reviewed the strategies that *don't* work, let's look at a simple step-by-step approach that *does* work:

Step 1. Make a list of all your sources of income: Social Security, pensions, lifetime annuities, or other reliable long-term income. Also do an inventory of all financial and real assets (stocks, bonds, mutual funds, CDs, real estate, rents, etc.) that can be used to fund your retirement.

Step 2. Estimate your monthly or annual expenses and divide them into essentials (food, housing, clothing, healthcare costs, insurance, gas, etc.) and discretionary (travel, entertainment, etc.).

Step 3. Compare your projected essential expenses with your projected total after-tax income. This comparison will either show that your essential expenses are fully covered, or it will reveal an essential expense gap that needs to be filled.

Step 4. If there is an expense gap, close the gap by either segregating a specific pool of assets to draw on systematically over time, or by purchasing a guaranteed income product, such as an immediate annuity. Once the essentials are funded, the remaining assets may be used for discretionary expenses.

Step 5. Review your plan with a financial professional at least once a year, adjusting all of the elements including expenses, asset allocation, and withdrawal rates, to address your changing personal circumstances.

Annuities can be a valuable part of a retirement income plan

As Americans live longer—twenty, thirty, or even forty years into retirement—and depend less on Social Security and defined benefits plans for income, the need for long-term income solutions is greater than ever. Annuities can provide safer, more stable retirement income.

"Longevity insurance annuities, also known as deferred income annuities, may provide part of the solution," reported Tom Streiff and Kristian Baney in *The Retirement Income Journal.* "At the same time, longevity insurance products don't easily fit the fee-based compensation structure toward which more advisors are moving. Simply put, fee-based advisors get paid based on assets under management, and pure longevity insurance isn't liquid, quantifiable asset. So, even those advisors who might believe longevity insurance is right for their clients must leave the managed account structure to purchase it."

A guaranteed minimum income benefit is designed to provide a guaranteed minimum of annuity payments by the insurance company, regardless of the performance of your annuity.

"I have always thought about [annuities with guarantees] as a way to put some sort of floor under an amount already saved by someone nearing retirement," said Michael Henkel, president of Envestnet/PMC.

Creating Plan B

Plan A is used when everything goes right. There are no mistakes. There are no problems with pensions, Social Security, or healthcare. Plan B is used when things don't work as planned. I used to watch *The A-Team* when I was growing up. The main character on the show never had just one plan entering a situation. He *always* had a backup plan.

If you don't have a backup plan for your retirement, you need to get one. One thing that is certain about retirement is that you can never foresee everything that is going to happen. Something will change between now and the end of your retirement, and you need to be ready.

Plan B has a lot to do with income because healthcare expenses, reductions in pensions, or Social Security payments are an issue for most people. Sometimes a retiree will take a single life payout of his pension and then die before his spouse. How can you create income after you die? In our firm, we are seeing this phenomenon more and more. If it doesn't result in a complete loss, the result is at least a partial loss of a pension. What is the Plan B to supplement income if a spouse dies sooner than expected?

For example, suppose an individual's retirement assets are $500,000 or more, and the person needs $18,000 of income per year or $1,500 per month? That is 3% interest. Should 3% interest be that difficult to replace? It shouldn't, but lately, we have seen it happen. Lately, people have been getting 1% on their accounts. How can you guarantee that your income will stay the same even if interest rates don't allow it? What about the circumstances around the world that affect our economy, such as the recent political situation in Egypt, as well as unrest in Greece,

Spain, and Portugal? We cannot do anything about these issues. It is what it is. Our office puts together a structured income plan or a Plan B for people who come to consult with us. Our clients decide they want a structured income plan—a plan that provides a 6% cash flow that is 92% tax-free. It allows you to continue to access your money without depleting your principal. This is a plan that lasts.

Some final thoughts about retirement income

Everyone should have a Plan B to protect and preserve their retirement income. Retirees should have a sound financial strategy for sustaining their income throughout retirement.

As the last decade has shown, the stock market is capable of disturbing even the best-laid plans. "Our research shows that retirees who take a 'set it and forget it' approach to their retirement income strategy do so at their own peril, particularly when hit by a bear market. Passively allowing markets to whipsaw your chances of having a successful retirement is not advisable. The past decade really shows the importance of revisiting your retirement income strategy regularly and making adjustments if necessary," explained Christine Fahlund, Senior Financial Advisor, T. Rowe Price Press, 2010.

Do you have a Plan B in case you face a reduction in your traditional sources of income? What if your CDs and other fixed income investments don't generate enough income? Do you have a backup plan? A comprehensive review by a trusted financial professional (such as our firm, conducted through our ARK program) can help you be more prepared to face your retirement income challenges.

A simple financial truth:
Income = Lifestyle

Chapter 6

Step 6:
Protect Yourself from a
Healthcare Crisis

The cost of a long-term healthcare crisis is skyrocketing, with no end in sight. Annual costs exceed $60,000—90,000 per year, and most of those costs are not covered by health insurance or Medicare.

In this chapter, you will learn:
- o Why affluent retirees have the most to lose
- o Why proper planning can save your assets
- o How to utilize an alternative Healthcare Plan and save thousands in premiums.

It is common sense to protect ourselves from the financial loss created by a car accident or house fire. However, few people appreciate the financial devastation of a long-term healthcare crisis. More disturbing is that even less people realize that there are other options of protecting themselves than long-term care insurance (which they may never use). Let me be clear: I am not saying that long-term care insurance is not wise for some people. For people with insufficient assets, it is the only logical decision. For most of our clients (who have over $500,000), there are better ways to use their assets in order to pay for their care if needed—without paying large fees to an insurance company.

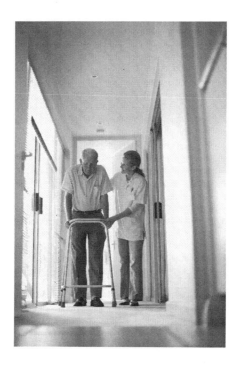

Why should you be concerned about a long-term healthcare crisis? Long-term healthcare is very expensive. According to recent studies, full-time nursing care for a loved one costs $5,000–10,000 per month, depending upon an individual's needs. A five-year nursing home stay can cost a family $300,000–600,000, and the cost is getting higher every year.

Still not concerned? Consider these facts: According to the American Healthcare Association, nearly half of all Americans will need some type of long-term healthcare before they die. The chances of such a crisis affecting you or your spouse is high. As people live longer, these odds increase. The cost of care also rises at an alarming rate. While cost of living increases for most retirees, the cost of healthcare has climbed to 7–10% per year, according to the Employee Benefit Research Institute (EBRI) in Washington, D.C.

I am often asked: "Doesn't Medicare cover these costs?" Unfortunately, except for the first 100 days (at less than 100%), the answer is no. What about Medicaid? Once again, if you have diligently saved over your lifetime, the answer is no. How about health insurance? Yet again—the answer is no. It doesn't matter how much you paid for traditional health insurance or how much tax you paid during your lifetime. If you have money, you won't get financial help from the government. You are on your own.

> *One of the biggest flaws for senior citizens in our country's healthcare system is that although they have paid taxes into the system, only the people who have no assets qualify for assistance. The system rewards people who haven't saved for their retirement and punishes the people who have saved.*

How can an affluent retiree protect his or her assets from being depleted by a long-term healthcare crisis? You have two basic options:

1. Buy long-term care insurance and transfer the risk to an insurance company
2. Leverage a portion of your assets to use in case you need them.

Traditional long-term care insurance works this way: You buy a certain amount of monthly benefits. If you suffer a healthcare crisis, the insurance company pays your expenses for a specified period. If you don't get sick, you lose what you paid in premiums. It's like car insurance—you have to crash to collect. How does a leveraged healthcare contingency plan work? Here's an example from one of our client files.

Joe and Judy are affluent retirees in their mid-sixties. They recently went through a long-term care crisis with Judy's mother. A five-year stay in a nursing home cost the family over $300,000. Joe and Judy have invested almost $1 million invested with our firm. They could fund a long-term care crisis directly from their accounts. However, they wanted to leave money to their children, grandchildren, church, and charity. An extended long-term healthcare crisis would severely deplete their nest egg. As an alternative to paying costly long-term care insurance premiums, we set up an account for $100,000 that would provide them with over $500,000 if either of them required long-term care. The best part of the plan was that if they didn't need to use it, either they or their loved ones would get back 100% (or more) of what they put into the account!

Another option we have successfully utilized is a new type of life insurance plan that contains an "Accelerated Benefit Payout for Long-Term Healthcare". In this type of plan, the insurance company agrees to pay out a portion of the death benefit before a person dies if they suffer a long-term healthcare crisis. For example, a $1,000,000 may pay out $300,000 or more in tax-free long-term care benefits if needed.

We have been able to help many of our clients save substantial amounts of money that they were paying in traditional long-term care insurance using some of these new alternative options. Additionally, many clients have been able to update existing life insurance policies to provide long-term care benefits at little to no additional cost. Our Ark program's comprehensive review can help you determine if one of these alternative options makes sense for you.

> *For most of our affluent clients, we don't*
> *recommend nursing home insurance...we help*
> *them develop plans to take care of themselves*
> *at home.*

"Healthcare in the U.S. is already under pressure from higher costs, and as baby boomers begin to retire, they will only add to the burden on healthcare in general and on Medicare in particular. Total expenditures are already exceeding $3 trillion dollars a year."

—Gregory Salsbury, PhD. *The American Retirement Crisis*, 2006.

Are you properly protected from a long-term healthcare crisis? Poor planning could cost you hundreds of thousands of dollars. Our ARK program can help you protect and preserve your assets from a financially devastating healthcare crisis.

—

Chapter 7

Step 7:
Make the Most Important
Financial Decision

The most important financial decision that you will ever make is the selection of your financial advisor. This choice will influence almost every other financial decision you make.

In this chapter, you will learn:
- How working with a financial professional benefits you
- What type of financial professionals exist
- How to select the right financial professional for you.

Should you be your own advisor?
Thinking you can be your own advisor is like asking a doctor to perform his own brain surgery. It's not impossible, I guess—but it's extremely dangerous!

Will you rely on what you can learn from reading books by Dave Ramsey or Suze Orman?

Before becoming a broker with Merrill Lynch, Suze Orman, the best-selling financial author and TV personality, was a waitress for the Buttercup Bakery in Berkeley, California. Why would Merrill Lynch hire a waitress? According to Ms. Orman:

"They weren't hiring a waitress. What they saw in me was that I would be an excellent saleswoman."

—Arthur Levitt, *Taking on the Street*

Maybe you get advice from *Money* magazine or another one of the financial publications that cover bookstore walls. "The rich are taking their advice from professional financial advisors. The poor are getting their advice from *Money* magazine," Robert Veres, financial author, explains.

Again, it is not impossible to find good, solid advice from books and magazines, but it can be very time-consuming—not to mention eye-straining.

You can watch hours of financial news programming every day: *CNBC, The Wall Street Report, Mad Money,* etc. Is it good information? Usually. Good entertainment? Often. Good for your marriage? Probably not!

The most logical choice is to find a highly qualified, well-seasoned, honest, ethical, and trusted financial advisor. You may think this sounds like an impossible task. Although I agree that it can be quite difficult to find a trusted advisor, our firm's thirty-year track record of clients comprised of people just like you tells me it can be done.

What are the different kinds of financial professionals?

Did you know that although there are over ninety different titles for financial professionals, the federal government only recognizes three? The three types of federally-recognized financial professionals are: Registered Representatives, Insurance Agents, and Investment Advisor Representatives. The following describes each group's capabilities and services.

Registered Representatives

The most common type of financial professional is called a Registered Representative (or stockbroker). Registered Representatives are regulated by Financial Industry Regulatory Authority (FINRA), which operates under the eyes of the Securities and Exchange Commission (SEC). All Registered Representatives must be employed by a FINRA Member Broker Dealer to sell financial products such as stocks, bonds, and mutual funds. In addition, Registered Representatives must hold a series G3 state license and either a Series 6 or Series 7 securities license.

FINRA calls a person who holds these licenses a Registered Representative because he or she is registered with FINRA and is a representative of the brokerage firm with which he or she is affiliated. Brokers are considered by FINRA and the SEC to be product salespeople whose job is to represent the best interests of their firms. According to the regulators, brokers sell investment products in order to earn commissions. They are not paid to give advice and any advice they do give is considered "incidental" to the sale of their products. In fact, the SEC requires that monthly statements issued by brokerage firms include the following disclosures: *Your account is a brokerage account and not an advisory account. Our interests may not always be the same as yours... Make sure you understand...the extent of our obligations to disclose conflicts of interest and to act in your best interest... Our salespersons' compensation may vary by product and over time.*

Registered Representatives make money by selling financial products that their broker dealer represents. The most common products sold are called *retail mutual funds*. With mutual funds, your money is pooled with other investors' money and managed by a fund manager. You are a shareholder, which grants you a proportionate share of the funds' gains, losses, and fees. Mutual funds charge shareholders fees in order to pay commissions and ongoing rewards to Registered Representatives.

The key point is that Registered Representatives—by license and employment contract—are commissioned-based salespeople.

> Commissions distort brokers' recommendations in many other ways. Some firms, for example, have special arrangements to sell mutual funds in exchange for above-average commissions. If a Merrill Lynch broker knows he'll get 25 percent more money for selling a Putnam mutual funds over an American Century fund, guess which fund the broker will try to sell you? Most large brokerage firms today sponsor their own funds, and may try to steer you to one of those. That way, the fee you pay to the manager of the mutual fund remains in-house and adds to the firm's profits. The problem is that brokerage firm funds don't necessarily perform better than, or even as well as, independent funds.

—Arthur Levitt, *Taking on the Street*

Insurance Agents

Another type of professional many people rely on for financial advice is an Insurance Agent. Every Insurance Agent must hold a state insurance license. An agent must hold a license based not on his state of residency, but on the residency of his clients. For example, if a New Jersey agent has clients who live in Delaware, the agent must hold a Delaware license. There are four main types of insurance licenses:

1. Property/Casualty license. Allows the agent to sell homeowners, automobile, and liability insurance.

2. Life/Health license. Allows the agent to sell life, health, accident, and disability income insurance, as well as fixed annuity products.

3. Long-Term Care Insurance license. Allows the agent to sell long-term care insurance.

4. Variable Annuity license. Allows the agent to sell variable annuity products, provided that the agent also holds the FINRA Series 6 or Series 7 licenses described earlier.

Insurance Agents' licenses (like stockbrokers' licenses) are held with one or more insurance companies. Agents (also like stockbrokers) legally represent the insurers, not their customers, as well as earn commissions from selling products. They do not earn fees for rendering advice.

"Captive" agents are employees of a particular insurance company. These agents sell that company's products only, similar to Ford salespeople selling only Ford automobiles.

"Independent" agents operate their own businesses or work for a general agent. Independent agents hold their licenses with many insurance companies, giving them access to a wider product line.

To make it even more complicated, some insurance companies employ their own agents while also allowing independent agents to sell their products.

Investment Advisor Representatives

Unlike Registered Representatives and Insurance Agents, an Investment Advisor Representative represents and works for you, rather than a Wall Street firm or insurance company. In fact, Investment Advisor Representatives have a "fiduciary duty" to serve your best interests. They have a legal responsibility to do what is best for you. This is in sharp contrast to a Registered Representative or Insurance Agents, whose primary duty is to their home office. An Investment Advisor Representative must hold one of the following FINRA licenses:

- **Series 65: Uniform Investment Adviser Law license.**
  Before practicing, the Investment Advisor Representative
  must also obtain a Series 63 state license.
- **Series 66: Uniform Combined State Law license.** This
  license combines the Series 65 and Series 63 into one
  examination.

The SEC regulates Registered Investment Advisory firms and
their Investment Advisor Representatives. Each state also regulates
Investment Advisor Representatives. In addition to passing
the necessary requirements to become an Investment Advisor
Representative, many of these advisors are also dually-licensed so
that they can help their clients with the investment and insurance
services they wish to obtain. This allows Investment Advisor
Representatives to provide holistic financial planning services to
their clients.

When you are in need of a trusted advisor, remember that there
are only three types of federal- and state-recognized advisors. Two of
the three types—Registered Representatives and Insurance Agents—
legally (by license) represent their company. They are paid on
commission to sell you their company's products. Investment Advisor
Representatives legally represent *you* and *your best interests*. They are
paid to *advise* and not to *sell*. Due to this distinction, most people pay
less fees to work with an Investment Advisor Representative rather
than a Registered Representative.

The Three Types of Federal & State Recognized Advisors

Advisor	Contractually Represents	Compensated By	Products Offered
Registered Representatives	A Broker Dealer	Selling Investment Products	*Limited to* Broker Dealer offerings
Insurance Agents	An Insurance Company	Selling Insurance Products	*Limited to* Insurance Company offerings
Registered Investment Advisors	The Client	Advising and Monitoring	*Unlimited* Access to most financial products and services

Choosing an Investment Advisory Firm

When you are looking for an Investment Advisory Firm, here are some key points to consider:

- The investment philosophy of the advisory firm should be consistent with your own. If you don't agree with their strategy for managing your money, don't use them.
- The firm should have a team with which you are comfortable. No individual has all the knowledge and skills necessary to assist someone over the entire financial spectrum. You may need advice at a time when one particular individual is not available. The firm should be committed to a team approach and you should meet the other advisors and staff that may work with you in the future.

- You should perform a careful due diligence on the firm and its principals. You should do a thorough reference check and make sure that both the firm and its individual members have the appropriate licenses. Most importantly, this due diligence should include a careful review of a document called the Form ADV. This form is required by the Investment Advisors Act of 1940 and must be filed with the regulatory body with which a Registered Investment Advisor (RIA) has registered (either the SEC or his or her state). The ADV is basically a disclosure document that sets forth information about the RIA, including the investment strategy, fee schedules, conflicts of interest, regulatory incidents, and so on. All RIAs are required to furnish new clients with either a Form ADV or another document containing similar information, in order to satisfy the "Brochure Rule" prescribed by the Act.
- The firm should be able to demonstrate to you that it can add value in a way that more than justifies its fees.

Some final thoughts about the value of a trusted advisor

Sound financial advice is worth the expense. An effective advisor can add value to your portfolio worth much more than his fee simply by preventing you from making very poor investment decisions (like chasing yesterday's hot sector).

It is my experience that many investors view fee structures from a mistaken perspective. They concern themselves with either the amount of time an advisor spends with them personally (effort) or the size of the fee (the lowest cost). Investors should be more concerned with how much value the advisor adds, relative to the cost. If the value exceeds the fee charged—even if the fee seems high at first—you will receive value. Conversely, if the value does not exceed the fee—no matter how low the fee—it is still too high.

Remember that good advice may not be cheap, but it is far less expensive than bad advice.

A startling fact: The total fees paid by a client utilizing a Registered Investment Advisor are often substantially less than the fee of a Registered Representative (Broker).

For more information, you can request our free report "How to Choose a Trusted Advisor" by visiting our website at www. theRetirementResource.org

Conclusion

The perfect financial storm is approaching fast. Those who don't prepare for it will most certainly suffer grave financial consequences. Those who do prepare for it will reap the rewards. The more a person owns, the more loss they risk. The old saying "You can't get blood out a rock" is very true. People with few assets and low income will not be affected as much as affluent savers and investors. If you are "rich" by the government's standards—meaning your annual income is $58,000 or more, and you own assets of $500,000 or more—seek a trusted financial advisory firm that utilizes a proven, systematic process (like our ARK program) to help you protect what you own and generate profit in the future.

Why traditional financial planning rarely works

The traditional financial planning process is treated by most advisors as an event, rather than a journey. You pay a fee—often quite substantial—to have your financial situation and goals assessed. Calculations are made to determine how much you need to invest. Then you are either on your own, or the advisor tries to sell you his company's financial products to complete your plan. At that point, you are free to monitor, update, and make any necessary corrections to your plan—unless you are willing to pay another financial planning fee and buy an additional company's products.

Our experience in reviewing prospective client's files is that this traditional approach rarely works. Once a financial plan has been paid for and the advisor has received his commission, the client is often deserted. Why? The advisor has earned the bulk of his money and there is little financial incentive for him to spend additional time with a client. Many clients are lucky if they hear from their financial advisor once a year, unless he is trying to sell them something. We believe that proper financial planning is not an event, but a *lifelong journey*. The original ark was the vehicle Noah used on his journey from danger to safety and prosperity; our ARK Financial Planning Process can be the vehicle to take you and your loved ones from your present financial situation to a reliable financial future.

Get Started with a Free Consultation

Your journey starts with a free consultation. Our consultation is designed to see if we can be of help to you and if we are able to accept you as a client. Due to the high level of ongoing service we provide, we can accept only a limited number of highly-valued clients. Should we both decide that we want to proceed, we will move to the next step.

What is the ARK program and how can it benefit me?

The ARK program is a unique financial planning strategy that we designed to protect our clients from the growing risks associated with the approaching financial storm, as well as to profit in the future. The ARK program utilizes a systematic approach to help our clients. We will:

1. Clarify your financial goals and concerns
2. Identify and address your financial risks
3. Establish a plan to reach your goals

4. Assist you in implementing all aspects of the plan, including coordinating, tax planning, legal documents, investments, and insurance.

When your personal ARK Financial Plan is built and implemented, what happens next?

Proper financial planning is a journey, not an event. We provide ongoing monitoring and updating of your program to make sure all aspects of the plan continue to achieve your financial objectives and properly address your financial concerns. We do so through our Advisory Membership Program, which puts us on retainer to keep your ARK plan on course.

What makes the ARK program different from other programs?

The key difference between our ARK program and the programs offered by most financial advisors around the country is that it has been personally designed for our clients. The ARK program is not a sales pitch designed by an investment or insurance company to promote its products and services. Our ARK program is the result of what we have learned from helping hundreds of clients over the past three decades. It is not created, owned, or funded by any investment or insurance company. It allows us, as Registered Investment Advisors, to create an unbiased plan of action that is customized to *you*. Most other financial plans simply lump all people into the same basic categories and recommend their company's products as the "solution". As Registered Investment Advisors, we get paid to advise, not to sell. We have no products to promote. This is the big difference between the ARK program and other programs.

Over the past thirty years, our firm has helped hundreds of people plan for a worry-free retirement. Through our ARK Financial Planning Process, we have helped our clients reduce their investment fees, avoid unnecessary taxes, protect their retirement accounts, maximize their returns, and establish a predictable source of supplemental income. I am sincerely happy for all of my wonderful clients.

However, I can't help think about the thousands of other people who have heard us speak in person, on TV, or on the radio, and decided not to take action. Some of them eventually decide to come in for a second opinion. Unfortunately, by then their situation is usually worse than it was when they first met us. Procrastination is a costly mistake when it comes to financial planning.

Now that you have reached the end of this book, I strongly encourage you to find a personal and trustworthy financial advisor and get your financial house in order. Should you wish to consider our firm, you can learn more about us at www.TheRetirementResource. org. Be sure to review our special offer for qualifying prospective clients on the next page!

We wish you a happy, healthy, and financially worry-free retirement!

Dave, DJ, and Jake Boike

A Special Free Offer to Readers of "High Tide: A Practical Guide for Affluent Retirees to Protect, Profit, and Prosper in the Approaching Storm"

We are so certain that we can be of tremendous help to qualifying prospective clients that we would like to offer you a free Ark Evaluation, with additional items currently valued at $598. This special offer includes:

- A one-hour consultation to address any financial questions or concerns
- An Ark Evaluation
- 3 months of our Platinum Advisory Membership newsletter
- 12 weeks of our Weekly Financial Update e-mails
- A copy of our *How to Choose a Trusted Financial Advisor* report
- 3 months of our DVD featuring important financial commentary directly from Dave.

To receive your special free offer valued at $598, simply call and schedule your free consultation within the next thirty days. You can do so at any time by calling Retirement Resources at (877) 732-5751, or by e-mailing Jake Boike at jakeboike@comcast.net.

Commonly Asked Questions

What are mutual funds?

A mutual fund is an investment company that pools money from shareholders and invests in a diversified portfolio of securities. An investor in a mutual fund is a shareholder who buys shares of the fund. Each share represents a proportionate ownership in all the fund's underlying securities.

What are index funds?

Index funds are designed to produce the same returns that investors would get if they owned all the stocks of a particular index. It is cost-prohibitive to own all the stocks of an index, unless, of course, the investor is a large institution. Thus private investors turn to index funds. There are many indexes; some of the better-known are listed here:

Dow Jones Industrial
Dow Jones Transportation
Russell 1000 Growth
Russell 1000 Value
Russell 2000 Value
Russell 3000

Russell Top 200 Growth
Russell Top 200 Growth
Standard and Poor's 100
Standard and Poor's 500
Standard & Poor's Midcap 400
Wilshire REIT (real estate)

Indexes are popular because the performances of the major stock and bond indexes often surpass the returns of mutual funds or managed money. In addition, they often have lower annual investment management costs. Index funds are considered "passive investing" because there is no active management (i.e., stock picking) involved; the fund manager simply purchases the stocks that make up the index the fund is supposed to track.

What are A-share mutual funds?

With A shares, the securities professional who sells the fund is paid a commission, on the front end, on the amount the client initially invests. They typical commission ranges from a low of 0 percent on investments of $1 million or more to a high of 5.75 percent on smaller investments. On larger investments, the broker or investment professional is paid a finder's fee at no cost to the client.

When a commission is paid, that amount is deducted from the investor's original investment. There is usually no additional charge to sell a front-end load fund.

What are B-share mutual funds?

Class B shares have contingent deferred sales charge (CDSC), or back-end load, instead of an initial sales charge.

The advisor or broker receives a 4 to 5 percent commission that is paid up front by the mutual fund company. To recover the commission it pays, the mutual fund company will impose a surrender or redemption charge when the investor liquidates the investment. The redemption charges gradually decline over the first several years of the investment. Once the mutual fund recovers the commission it paid to the sales professional, the Class B share will often convert to a

Class A share, which usually has lower management fees. In addition, B shares typically have a 12b-1 annual charge (generally 1percent) that enables the fund to recoup the up-front sales charge.

With some mutual funds, a shareholder can systematically withdraw up to 12 percent of the investment's value from the B share fund without any charge.

What are Class C shares?

Class C mutual fund shares have either a minimal front-end or back-end sales charge (typically 1 percent) or no front-end or back end charge. Instead of paying a front-end commission to the broker or advisor, the mutual fund company pays an annual commission of around 1percent from the annual management fees it charges the investors.

Is there a difference in performance between A, B, and C shares?

A mutual fund company may offer separate funds with the same name, same objectives, and same manager that differ only by how the load is paid. For instance, there may be an XYZ Fund A, XYZ Fund B, and XYZ Fund C. The difference in their returns is solely attributable to the expenses deducted from the funds.

What are Y-share, or institutional-class, mutual funds?

A number of mutual funds limit their availability to large institutional investors, such as pension funds, or to high-net-worth individuals through registered investment advisors. Since they do not have to deal with the public, their internal costs are generally lower than those of equivalent "retail" mutual fund, and they pass this cost savings along to the investors.

A Y-share mutual fund is distinguished by the high minimum deposit required upon original purchase. The amount usually starts at $1million and can go as high as $5 million per investor. Y-share funds are referred to as institutional funds because larger institutions, such as financial advisory firms, pension and profit sharing plans, and other large investors, can better afford the minimum required investment.

There are no front-end or back-end charges on these funds. Their expense ratios range from .20 and .70 percent.

Investors who do not have enough funds to meet the minimums required for Y shares can invest in them through their brokerage firm or registered advisory firm. These firms purchase Y share funds as part of a managed mutual fund account for which they charge a management fee of about 1percent.

In some cases, institutional funds may be available through discount brokers. Discount brokers typically require that the fund increase its expenses by .25 percent. This increase is then paid to the discount brokerage firm to allow the investor to buy it with no transaction costs.

What do mutual funds charge for managing my money?

Mutual funds charge a management fee and an administration fee. The management fee is typically .5 to 1percent and is paid to the management firm for making the buy and sell decisions for the securities in the fund. The administration fee is related to the costs for annual reports, prospectuses, accounting audits and reports, and so on. This fee ranges from .1to .15 percent.

Some funds, whether load or no-load, charge additional fees called 12b-1fees to pay for marketing and advertising expenses or, more commonly, for compensating sales professionals and advisory firms. By law 12b-1fees cannot exceed .75 percent of the fund's average net assets per year; they are typically closer to .25 percent.

The total of all three fees is the expense ratio, which on average for all funds will run about 1.35 to 1.5percent on an annual basis.

The commissions for trading the securities within the fund are not reported in the expense ratio and can add an additional .1to 1 percent to the total expense. These fees are calculated and deducted from the mutual fund daily.

What is an annuity?

An annuity is a contract between an investor and an insurance or investment company in which the investor makes a lump-sum investment or a series of investments in exchange for a stream of income in the future. Annuities can be set up to provide a guaranteed income for life.

What are the primary types of annuities?

The two primary types of annuities are immediate annuities and tax-deferred annuities. An immediate annuity is one in which an initial investment is made and annuity payments start immediately at a fixed interest rate over a period of years, for the life of the annuity owner, or for the life of the owner and another person (joint and survivor annuity), usually the owner's spouse. With immediate annuities, the owner cannot take out the investment as a lump sum, and once the annuitization method of distribution has been chosen, it cannot be changed.

Tax-deferred annuities allow income earned on investments to accumulate free from tax. Taxes on the earnings are paid when they are taken out, not as they are earned. In a deferred annuity, the owner retains control over how the annuity is invested and how and when the annuity proceeds are paid out.

Because of the tax-benefits and increased control, tax deferred annuities are much more popular than immediate annuities. Within the tax-deferred type of annuity, annuities are further classified as fixed, variable, or indexed, according to the underlying investment structure of the annuity.

Can you explain how a fixed annuity works?

With a fixed annuity, the investment company guarantees the principal against loss and guarantees a specific rate of return per year or per time period. Earnings accumulate on a tax-deferred basis until withdrawn. Fixed annuities usually pay slightly higher rates than do Treasure bills or COs.

The interest rate with most fixed annuities will change on a year-to-year basis but is usually guaranteed not to go below a specific rate, such as 3 or 4 percent. Some fixed annuities will change on a year-to-year basis but is usually guaranteed not to go below a specific rate, such as 3 or 4 percent. Some fixed annuities lock in a fixed rate of return for a 3-, 4-, 5-, or 6-year time span.

What is a variable annuity?

A variable annuity has most of the features of a fixed annuity with one major difference: The investor chooses the investments within the annuity, which can be a combination of fixed and variable investments.

While the rate of return on a fixed annuity is guaranteed by the insurance, or investment, company, the rate of return on a variable annuity is based on the success of the investments chosen by the investor. The investor has the right to place money into various subaccounts such as stocks, bonds, balanced portfolios, growth, growth income, and sector areas (e.g., international, health, financial services, banking, gold, energy, technology). The investor can split the total investment inside the annuity to diversify and balance the risk. Variable annuities are riskier than fixed annuities because there is not guaranteed rate of return. Most variable annuities offer a guaranteed of the original investment only if the investor dies before taking distributions.

As with the fixed annuity, the investor does not pay taxes on the income ore growth until he or she withdraws it.

Can you explain indexed annuities?
Indexed annuities are a cross between fixed annuities and variable annuities. In addition to offering guaranteed principal and usually a small 2 or 3 percent rate of return as a floor, they also offer the investor the ability to participate in the upside of potential of an index such as the popular S&P 500.

The investor receives a specific guaranteed rate of return on his or her investment over a short time period, ranging from 1to 5 years, although it can be longer. If the S&P 500 index is higher at the end of this time period than it was when the annuity began, the investor will receive a certain percentage (60 to 90 percent) of the gain. If the S&P 500 index is lower than it was when the investment started, the investor loses nothing-the indexed annuity guarantees there can be no loss or participation in the downside of the index.

There are numerous types of indexed annuities, but the two most prevalent are point-to-point and year-to-year annuities. A point-to-point indexed annuity has the S&P 500 index pricing start on the day of purchase and continue to the termination of the plan. Fluctuations in the S&P 500 index that occur between those two points have no bearing on the rate of return. The return is based only on a comparison between the start date and the termination date. Many companies now have websites on the Internet that you can visit to obtain or request information.

For more detailed information, you can ask your financial advisor or broker to do some research for you.

What are investment rating services for mutual funds?

There are several rating services that are considered the leaders in the United States. Lipper Analytical and Morningstar rate and rank the mutual funds available in the marketplace. They discuss, in great detail, previous results, charges, fees and costs, the history of the company, the portfolio manager and its management makeup, the risk involved, and the goals of the firm. Their data are based on previous results and future projections.

Although rating services are an important source of information for an investor, they should not be the only decision making tool used in choosing a mutual fund.

What is a managed brokerage account?

Financial advisory brokerage firms provide managed accounts for clients who want to have a stock or bond account managed on a discretionary basis. With a managed account, you delegate the responsibility for selecting investments to the financial advisor or stockbroker. The professional advisor assists you in establishing an investment policy statement and then will search through hundreds of investments to match your objectives. Stocks, bonds, mutual funds, certificates of deposit, and any other traditional brokerage product can be purchased in the account.

Many private management firms do not accept accounts under $10 million. However, there are also many financial advisory and brokerage firms that have arrangements for accounts to be established for a minimum investment of $250,000.

What are the fees for managed accounts?

A managed account is simply a traditional brokerage account, except the investor does not pay commissions. A management fee, typically 2 percent for smaller accounts but as low as .5 percent for larger accounts (i.e. over $3 million), is charged by the financial advisor or broker on the value of the account. All transaction costs and money manager, custodian, and advisors' fees are inclusive in one fee.

My financial advisor recommends that I set up an account with a brokerage firm that will hold all my mutual funds and other investments and will manage them for an annual fee. Is this a managed account?
Yes.

What are tax-advantaged investments?

Investments such as Treasury bonds, bills, and notes, whose interest is subject only to federal income tax, have slight tax advantages. Investments in some real estate, equipment leases, and energy programs provide income tax advantages due to pass through of depreciation, depletion, and tax-deductible expenses. Tax-deferred annuities, discussed earlier, also fall into the category of tax-advantaged investments.

What are tax-exempt investments?

Tax-exempt investments are investments that generate income that is exempt from federal taxes. Municipal bonds are the most common tax-exempt investments. Municipal bonds issued by your state of residence are also not subject to state income taxes.

Generally, the yield of tax-exempt investments is lower than that of corporate bonds. However, since the income is tax-free, the lower yield of tax-exempt investments for investors with high income is typically greater than the after-tax yield of equivalent taxable investments.

What is investment planning?

Investment planning is a process that helps you systematically build and implement a sound investment plan. It has seven levels and is often depicted as a pyramid.

1. Objectives: In establishing objectives, you define why you are investing and where you want your investment plan to lead.

2. Risk Tolerance: At this level, you define your defensive posturing to protect your plan from the uncontrollable risks that investing creates. Your financial advisor will work with you to identify your tolerance to all the risks involved in investing.

3. Buying policy: You must develop a dominant buying policy. This policy will drive and direct the type of investments that you or your advisors but into and sell out of your portfolio.

4. Asset allocation policy: Your asset allocation policy is developed in conjunction with your buying policy. It determines the categories of assets in which you will invest to meet your investment goals while staying within your risk tolerance.

5. Management policy: Your management policy outlines the expectations you have about, and the interaction you expect to have with, the professionals who are acting on your behalf throughout the investment process.

6. Taxation: It is prudent to include a taxation level of control within your plan. This level requires that you and your advisors address the obvious tax ramifications and effects that your investment earnings can have on your overall financial situation. The impact of taxation can be controlled and minimized with proper design of your portfolio and comprehensive asset-management.

7. Asset selection: At the final level of your investment pyramid, you select the assets that will constitute your investment portfolio. Although many investors begin the planning process by selecting the assets they would like to purchase, this is often misguided. In reality, the selection of the securities that will compile a portfolio is not the foundation but the capstone of a well-designed and -implemented investment plan.

What is the key to a successful investment program?

Investing without objectives can be very difficult, haphazard, and dangerous. The key to a successful investment program is to develop (1) your financial goals and objectives, then (2) the overall financial plan to achieve those goals with economic security, and then (3) an investment plan within the context of your financial plan.

Having concrete financial goals is the foundation for planning your financial future. Your investment plan is the implementation of buying and investing strategies that will help fulfill your financial plan. Rather than thinking about financial planning as a one-time activity, think of it as process or a series of steps that will lead to the attainment of your financial goals.

An investment program may encompass different investment vehicles, each with its own risk and reward characteristics. Successful investment plans employ various strategies designed to either increase the rate of return on the investment or reduce its risk. Self-assessment and the use of a monitoring system that incorporates periodic evaluation in light of changing market conditions complete the process.

Why is an investment strategy important?

Every serious endeavor should begin with a strategy or plan aimed at getting you to your chosen goal. A strategy focused our attention and energies on those actions that systematically move us closer to our financial objectives, and it helps us tune out the many distractions that dissipate that attention and energy.

Strategy is critical in warfare, in business management, and, yes, in investment planning. The investor who lacks a strategy reacts with undifferentiated attention to every unanticipated event; before long, he or she is going everywhere, but not anywhere in particular.

What are the elements of an investment strategy?

An investment strategy is dependent upon three key elements:

1. An identifiable goal
2. A method to attain that goal
3. The competencies and resources to sustain the strategy

The investment strategy must operate within the framework of the client's investment policy (discussed later in this chapter) and must always be its servant.

What is the monitoring step?

The financial advisor monitors the performance of investments, changes in the tax law, and the general economic environment and keeps the client posted through periodic meetings. These meetings should be two-way exchanges of information: the investment professional reports facts and insights relative to the client's investment program; at the same time, the investment professional reports facts and insights relative to the client's investment program; at the same time, the investment professional attempts to determine if any material changes have taken place in the client's financial situation, investment outlook, or attitude toward risk. This dialog, in effect, provides the feedback loop to the initial steps of the investment management process.

How do I most effectively work with my financial advisor to set my investment goals?

Your financial advisor must be thoroughly acquainted with your personality, your health, and your family situation, including your dependents, any special needs, the income that is needed from the portfolio, income from outside sources, and your marginal income tax rate.

Your investment constraints should be addressed. These may include industries or companies in which you do not want to invest, such as tobacco or liquor; liquidity and the need for it now and in the future; and legal constraints, such as the legal form of the investing entity (is it a trust, an irrevocable trust, a charitable trust?). Your time horizon must be discussed, not only in terms of your age or life expectancy but also in terms of legal entity.

Typical investment objectives include financial independence, retirement, college education funding, purchase of a new car or home, improved lifestyle, and tax reduction.

You and your advisor should collaborate to put in writing the factors that make up your entire financial picture. From this information gathering come the factors that are important to you, such as your objectives, your return expectations, your risk preferences, and the real and perceived level of your wealth.

Once my financial advisor and I have determined my investment personality, what then?

Your investment personality leads to the investment policy statement (IPS), in which your investment planning objectives are translated into a portfolio strategy. The IPS states the fundamental goals and objectives regarding how you want to invest your funds and sates how those goals and objectives will be achieved.

The major reasons for developing an IPS are to foster clear communication between you and your investment advisor and to enable you and your advisor to protect the portfolio from ad hoc revisions to your long-term goals should short-term conditions become distressing and cause you to start second guessing your policy.

What specific issues should be addressed in my IPS?

At a minimum your IPS should provide for:

•   Investment objectives, including your rate-of-return objectives, risk tolerance, time horizon or investment holding period, income needs, and economic assumptions.

•   Asset allocation plan, including primarily asset class preferences and the total percentage of the portfolio that can be allocated to a given asset class. Asset classes will include a larger cap, small cap, international, bonds, and cash, but these classes can be expanded to include more or to be more specific.

• Guidelines for choice of assets, allowing you to specifically exclude a type of stock or a specific stock from the portfolio.

• Process for selecting funds and/or fund managers, including the minimum requirements for being included for consideration.

• Investment expectations, outlining rate-of-return expectations within the context of factors such as inflation, taxes, power of compounding, risk-return trade-off, and diversification.

• Review procedures: establishing how performance will be reported, what benchmarks will be used for measurement, and the frequency of meetings.

What are the advantages of indexing?

Indexing, or passive investing, involves buying an investment product that contains the entire basket of stocks that make up an index or asset class. Proponents of indexing see the following advantages of using this investment strategy:

1. Indexing results in increased diversification and avoids fund manager risk.
2. Indexing results in lower implementation costs since the purchase is executed with mutual or pooled funds whose administrative and transaction costs are shared among all investors.

3. Passive investing offers certainty in matching the risk-reward profile and performance measurement standards established in an investor's investment policy statement.
4. Given the lack of active management in indexed funds, there is less turnover and thus they tend to be more tax-efficient.

What are some advantages of annuities?

Tax advantages and the need for baby boomers to save more efficiently for retirement are the main reasons the sales of annuity products have skyrocketed. Qualified plans have a ceiling for contributions, built-in "reverse discrimination" because of coverage requirements, and complex red tape. Many individuals, retirees, and employers have turned to tax-deferred annuities to supplement their retirement savings to lower their annual exposure to taxable interest and investment gain. Listed below are some of the advantages of annuities:

1. Unless the annuity is owned by a for-profit corporation or other entity, all income and growth is tax-deferred until it is withdrawn.
2. By reallocating taxable investments to deferred annuity investments, it is possible for an individual to lower taxable income each year and thus the taxes he or she pays. A retiree with a large amount of taxable interest income can reallocate assets to annuities and potentially reduce or eliminate the tax liability he or she pays on Social Security benefits.
3. When distributions are made, taxable interest or gain comes out on a pro rata basis.
4. The beneficiary designation on the annuity allows the proceeds or death benefit to be paid directly to the designated beneficiary without having to go through probate.
5. On the death of the annuity owner, the owner's spouse, if he or she is the beneficiary, can roll the annuity contract over

into his or her own name and the tax deferral will be retained. All other beneficiaries must elect to annuitize the benefit within 1 year of the owner's date of death or to take the total amount in one distribution or in a series of even or uneven distributions within 5 years from the date of death of the deceased.

6. The owner of the annuity can choose between guaranteed investment accounts or the many types of variable subaccounts. The subaccounts include, but are not limited to, stock, bond, balanced, specialty, and international investments. The insurer behind the annuity offers professional management and subaccounts. The owner can transfer between these accounts at will without incurring a taxable event.

7. About two-thirds of the states offer at least some creditor protection for annuities.

What are some disadvantages of annuities?

Some disadvantages of annuities are:

1. Compared with other investment vehicles, none of the taxable income or growth from an annuity is taxed at the favorable capital gain rate.

2. Annuities have higher administration costs compared with other investment vehicles, as well as mortality and expense changes, that with hypothetical comparisons of the performance of the annuity and that of mutual funds.

Whether you should own mutual funds or variable annuities, or a combination of the two, depends upon your individual circumstances. A thoughtful evaluation should be performed before you make a decision.

If I'm disappointed with the performance of my existing annuity, can I replace it with a more competitive annuity?

Yes. It is common to replace one annuity with another. However, such an exchange should be done only after a careful comparison of the advantages and disadvantages.

If you decide to make the exchange, be sure that the transfer is done directly between the existing annuity company and the new annuity company. By meeting this requirement, among others, you comply with Section 1035 of the Internal Revenue Code, which allows the tax-free exchange of one annuity for another. Without the protection of Section 1035, income taxes would be due on the accumulated gain in your existing annuity.

By using the "1035 transfer" method, can I consolidate several annuities into one new annuity account?

It depends. Many annuity companies will not permit you to consolidate several annuities and protect your transferred tax deferral. Others will. Make sure you are working with a financial advisor who thoroughly the financials for each one. To obtain the most accurate financial numbers, get a copy of the part of the seller's tax return that pertains to the property. It will have the property's income and expenses. You should then prepare a second income and expense form to include your adjustments, such as a reasonable vacancy factor, probable increases in property taxes (due to sale), potential debt service (mortgage payments), and any other adjustments you think are reasonable.

Use your reconstructed 1-year analysis as a basis for projecting various future cash flows and the potential future sale price. These numbers should all be adjusted for taxes (including the savings from depreciation) to get to the bottom line. The final numbers will help you determine your overall rate of return, which is often referred to as the internal rate of return (IRR).

Don't forget to include a management fee when calculating your cash flows. Any good financial calculator can help you compute the IRR, which is the best way for you to compare different types of investments.

You can achieve success in all your real estate investments by making a careful analysis of the location, the structural soundness, the management requirements, and the return as projected by your IRR calculations.

What are the advantages of investing through a managed account?

A managed account has a number of advantages. First, there is no incentive for the broker to "churn" the account to generate commissions, since there are none. Second, the financial advisor or broker is paid to continue a high level of service and to be actively involved in guiding you toward the attainment of your goals. Your success and the professional's success are tied together.

What are the penalties I need to be concerned about with the regard to retirement plan distributions?

You need to be careful of running into what is sometimes referred to as the "Goldilocks" problem. You remember the story of the three bears, where the porridge was too hot and too cold. With retirement plan assets, the problems to watch out for when taking distributions are too soon, too little, too late.

- Too soon: If distributions are taken before age 59 Y2, these are called early distributions.
- Too little: At age 70 Y2, minimum distributions are required each year. This is the absolute minimum required distribution

amount, there is a 50 percent penalty on the difference between what should have been withdrawn and what was withdrawn.

- Too late: The first minimum distribution is required to be taken by April 1of the calendar year after the year in which one reaches 70 Y2. Thereafter, the minimum distributions have to be taken within each calendar year, or there is a 50 percent penalty on the amount not taken that year.

What are the rules regarding distributions from traditional IRAs?

You can withdraw money from your IRA at any time and pay income tax on the amounts withdrawn. However, because your IRA is intended to be a long-term investment, unless certain exceptions are met, withdrawals before age 59 Y2 are subject to a 10 percent penalty. The 10 percent penalty is in addition to the income taxes due on the total amount of the withdrawals.

On the other end of the spectrum, you are required to take distributions from traditional IRAs on your "required beginning date." Failure to do so can result in significant penalties.

What is the required beginning date, and when is it?

The required beginning date is April 1of the calendar year after you turn 70 Y2. However, you are allowed to postpone your first distribution until the following tax year, but doing so sometimes creates an inadvertent income tax problem. This is because the second distribution will be in the same tax year as the first distribution, most likely pushing you into a higher marginal tax bracket than necessary. In most cases, bunching the two distributions into one year would not be prudent, unless you had significant tax write-offs for that year. Thus, even though you can postpone your first required distribution, check with your tax advisor before you do so, or the postponement may cost you additional tax dollars.

With the exception of the postponement rule, for all other years, IRA distributions need to occur by December 31. Failure to make timely distributions is subject to penalties.

What are the distribution rules for Roth IRAs?

You can take money out of your Roth IRA at any time, just as with a traditional IRA. Unlike the case with a traditional IRA, however, you will not pay income tax on withdrawals of your contributions. Any amounts you withdraw from a Roth IRA are deemed first to be contributions up to the aggregate total of all contributions to all Roth IRAs. Only after you have taken all contributions are distributions considered to be distributions of your earnings. You also will not pay income tax on the distributions of your accumulated earnings if they are part of a qualified distribution. If the distribution of your accumulated earnings is not a qualified distribution, you will pay income tax and possible a penalty on the earnings you withdraw.

Does the 10 percent penalty tax apply to my Roth IRA?

Yes. The 10 percent penalty tax on distributions before 59 Y2 generally applies to all IRAs, including Roth IRAs. However, this penalty applies only to certain withdrawals from Roth IRAs, which are discussed in detail in this chapter.

When do I have to begin taking distributions from my qualified retirement plan?

You must begin taking minimum required distributions from a qualified plan by April 1of the calendar year following the year in which you turn 70 Y2 unless you qualify for deferring distributions. This rule applies to all qualified plans, including 403(b) and 401(k) plans.

Is it possible to take penalty-free distributions from a traditional IRA before turning 59 Y2?

All early distributions from a traditional IRA are subject to a 10 percent penalty unless an exception applies. An early distribution is any distribution taken before the owner reaches 59 Y2 years of age. There are eight exceptions to this rule for traditional IRAs:

1. The owner dies before reaching age 59 Y2, and the distribution goes to a beneficiary or the owner's estate.
2. The IRA owner becomes totally and permanently disabled.
3. Distributions are part of a series of substantially equal periodic payments.
4. Distributions are for higher-education expenses for the IRA account owner or his or her spouse, children, or grandchildren.
5. Distributions are for medical expenses that exceed 7.5 percent of the IRA owner's adjusted gross income.
6. Distributions are for health insurance premiums for the account owner of his or her spouse and dependents after the account owner has become unemployed.
7. Distributions are used by first-time home buyers for expenses up to a $10,000 lifetime cap.
8. A qualified rollover to another IRA is made.

What is a qualified rollover?

A rollover is the process of rolling funds from one type of account to another without paying any income tax. Allowable rollovers include:

- Rollovers from one traditional IRA to another traditional IRA
- Rollovers from an employer-sponsored qualified plan to a traditional IRA

You cannot roll over a traditional IRA to a Roth IRA tax-free, and you cannot roll over from a qualified plan to a Roth IRA at all.

What is a lump-sum option?

Many plans offer a lump-sum option, which allows the employee to take one-time cash benefit and leave the plan. The employee can either take the benefit in cash and pay income taxes on it or transfer the funds to an IRA pay taxes on the funds when they are eventually withdrawn. In many cases an employee can assume the risk and create a larger retirement income benefit by transferring the funds to an IRA and properly investing the proceeds.

What are the tax rules relating to lump-sum distributions of retirement funds?

Lump-sum distributions can be rolled over (in whole or in part) to an IRA on a tax-free basis. Alternatively, employees can take the lump sum in cash and either pay the entire tax due or use 10-year forward averaging, if available, for paying taxes.

What is an IRA rollover?

An IRA rollover is a lump-sum distribution from a qualified plan deposited into a special IRA account. The employee can deposit the distribution himself or herself or the employer can transfer it directly.

Rollover IRAs are popular because they offer substantial benefits. The money in the IRA continues to grow tax-deferred in investments that can be controlled by the IRA owner, and there is flexibility in how and when distributions are taken.

What do I need to know if I want to do a rollover to an IRA from a qualified plan?

If you decide on a direct rollover to an IRA, make sure you have an IRA set up so that the transfer is done correctly. If you do not have an existing IRA, you must open one. Whether it's a new IRA or an old one, you should meet with your financial advisor and fill out the proper forms so that the funds are transferred correctly. Failure to do so can result in many problems, creating an unnecessary tax liability and/or having the plan administrator withhold taxes when what you are trying to accomplish is a tax-free exchange.

After I leave my job, should I leave my 401(k) retirement account at work and take an annuity or roll over the account to an IRA?

Although you could certainly leave your 401(k) proceeds at work, doing so may not be a good idea for various reasons. Like any other retirement plan decision, there are pros and cons.

On the positive side, many of the fees inside a 401(k) plan are less than the fees outside the plan. In addition, you may be able to sell the stock within the stock account-assuming that you have one in your 40l(k) plan-without incurring significant expense, such as commissions.

However, the negative consequences of leaving money in a 401(k) plan usually outweigh the positive reasons for keeping it in. The average number of investment alternatives in a 401(k) plan is seven.

Should you roll your money out of your 401(k) and into a self-directed IRA, you will have virtually unlimited investment choices-stocks, bonds, mutual funds, stock options, and possibly even real estate, as well as other investments. Also, most 401(k) plans typically have only one or two specific types of investments in each broad investment category. There may be only one large-cap equity fund, for example. If you roll your 401(k) money into an IRA, you will have many alternatives. In annuity election that is properly made, by its own terms, meet the required minimum distribution rules.

Must I take all my money out of my traditional IRA when I reach 70 Y2?

You do not have to take all the money out of your IRA when you reach 70 Y2, but you are required to take an annual minimum amount, called the required minimum distribution. However, you can still take as much as you want from your IRA at any time as long as you are prepared to pay the taxes on the amounts withdrawn.

What happens if I don't begin taking required minimum distributions after I turn age 70 Y2?

Required minimum distributions must start no later than the required beginning date. If you do not take them, you will be assessed a penalty of 50 percent on the difference between what you took and what was required to be taken.

For example, if your minimum distribution is $10,000 and you take only $4,000, you are $6,000 short. Your penalty will be $3,000, in addition to income taxes that may be due. Talk about a mistake!

What is the actual required beginning date?

The required beginning date, as defined in the Internal Revenue Code, is April 1 of the calendar year following the individual's attainment of age 70 Y2. In most instances, an individual participating in a qualified retirement plan who does not own more than 5 percent of the plan's sponsor as of age 66 Y2, directly or by attribution, can defer receiving benefits until April 1of the calendar year following actual retirement.

How do I calculate the minimum distribution once I designate a beneficiary and select the payout option?

Publication 590, "Individual Retirement Arrangements," which can be obtained from the Internal Revenue Service, provides a divisor based on the age of an individual or on joint lives. You divide the fair market value of your IRA as of December 31of the year that you turn age 70 Y2 by the appropriate divisor. The result is your minimum distribution requirement.

For example, a 70- and 65-year old have a joint life expectancy of 23.1years. If your IRA is worth $200,000, divide $200,000 by 23.1to determine your minimum distribution ($8,658.01). This is your minimum distribution for the first year. The required minimum distribution for each year thereafter will be determined by the calculation method you choose.

How will I be taxed on my pension benefit?

Benefits received from a qualified retirement plan are subject to income tax for the year in which they are received.

How does the spousal IRA rollover work?

After the plan participant's death, the surviving spouse has the option to roll the assets of each retirement plan over to an IRA. Although the spouse could roll over the retirement plan assets into his or her own existing IRA, it is usually best to establish a new, separate spousal rollover account.

What are the advantages of a spousal rollover?

A spousal rollover enables the surviving spouse to establish new distribution options, such as naming children as designated beneficiaries and using the MDIB table to create stretch-out possibilities.

Is it possible to designate a trust as beneficiary of an IRA or other tax-deferred retirement account without losing the advantages of lifetime tax deferral for a nonspouse beneficiary?

Yes. With careful planning and coordination of trust provisions and beneficiary designations, a trust can qualify as a designated beneficiary receiving plan distributions for the trust beneficiaries and continuing tax deferral on amounts not paid out from the plan. If multiple beneficiaries are named in the trust, the life expectancy of the oldest trust beneficiary is used for calculating required minimum distributions to the trust. The trust must meet the designated-beneficiary rules for trusts, as described above.

Should I transfer the title of ownership of my IRAs into my living trust now?

Absolutely not! Transferring title or ownership of IRAs or other retirement accounts to a living trust creates an immediate income taxable event on the entire balances. You only change the beneficiary designation of your IRAs and other retirement plans to the name of your living trust. You should seek proper professional advice before naming your living trust as a beneficiary of these accounts.

Also, be sure you have a durable general power of attorney as part of your estate plan. Thus, if you become disabled, the person you name as your attorney-in-fact under this power can access these accounts even though they are not titled in the trust's name. This may be important in order to avoid unnecessary taxes and penalties for failure to make minimum required distributions.

I've heard that I can stretch out the payout from my IRA over my and then my children's life expectancies. Why would I want to do this?

Flipping or stretching out an IRA is a planning strategy that enables your beneficiaries to keep money in your IRA for as long as possible after your death. The longer the plan assets remain in the tax deferred account, the greater the tax-free accumulation. Tax-free accumulation and income-tax deferral combine to greatly increase the value of the account for children or grandchildren.

Can I leverage an IRA tax deferral into multigenerational wealth?

If there is a sufficient amount of other assets to fully fund a husband's and wife's applicable exclusion amounts, the spouses should consider using the husband's IRA to create a multigenerational tax shelter. The husband should name his wife as the beneficiary of his IRA so that if she survives him, she can make a spousal IRA rollover. She could then apply the flip/stretch-out strategy to designate children, grandchildren, or trusts for the children and grandchildren as beneficiaries. This approach allows the husband's IRA money to retain its tax-deferred status for a substantial period of time after both the husband and wife are deceased.

Another alternative is to convert the traditional IRA to a Roth IRA and name the grandchildren as the beneficiaries. This assumes, of course, that the funds are available to pay the income taxes in the year of the conversion.

What is an eternal IRA?

An eternal IRA, also referred to as a dynasty IRA or stretch IRA, is an IRA for which the account owner names grandchildren as beneficiaries to stretch the payout period as long as possible and maintain the retirement assets for the ultimate use of the grandchildren-and perhaps even great-grandchildren. If grandchildren are to be the beneficiaries and one or more of them are minors, be sure to name a guardian or custodian in the beneficiary designation and not the grandchild directly.

Generation-skipping transfer (GST) tax issues also come into play. The IRA transfer cannot convey more than $1 million to grandchildren or lower generations without incurring a GST penalty tax.

With careful planning, an irrevocable trust for the benefit of grandchildren may be named as the beneficiary, thereby providing additional asset protection benefits.

Is the eternal IRA a planning technique that my IRA custodian would know about?

The eternal IRA is a sophisticated planning idea. Many, if not most, IRA custodians are not in the business of planning; they are in the business of managing assets. So it is not likely that your custodian will inform you of this technique or help you to make the proper elections.

If your custodian does not know about this technique, you should insist that he or she find out about it. You should also be working with a financial advisor who is well versed in this technique. If it is a technique that fits your planning goals, you and your advisor can them work with your custodian to ensure that the proper elections are made and the plan is put in place.

How are IRAs, qualified plans, and annuities taxed at death?

If assets are owned in an IRA, qualified plan, or annuity at the time of the owner's death, there will be more than one tax on their value. Distributions from these plans trigger taxable income to the recipients. Such distributions are referred to as income in respect of a descendent, or IRD. Since these assets are also included in their owner's taxable estates the assets are also subject to federal estate tax.

A True Story Regarding Client Relationships

Have you ever done something for someone that you thought was just routine, but later found out that you had made a real difference in that person's day? Maybe you called a friend or family member just to say, "Hi", without knowing that that person was dealing with some difficult circumstances and you ended up being a great source of comfort or encouragement. Maybe you sent a thank you card to someone who did something for you, without knowing that the person had just dealt with a string of people who were anything but appreciative.

Didn't it make you feel good when that person told you how much your call or card or what you did meant to them? I recently had another of these experiences with one of our Member Clients. In order to preserve privacy, let's call the Member Client "Bob". Bob and his wife came in to see me in the fall of 2009. They had been referred to me by another client.

Bob and his wife were retired former business owners who had just lost a significant portion of their retirement nest egg during the 2008 Market Crash. Their former advisor provided no guidance as their account values dropped like a rock, according to Bob.

Then when they called in and requested a review in early 2009, all their advisor said was, "don't worry about it...just hang on, the markets always go back up eventually".

That's when Bob and his wife knew it was time for a change. This was their life savings, and this was their time to be enjoying the fruits of their labors, not worrying about losing money. After several meetings, Bob and his wife decided they wanted to become our Clients. Within days we had identified areas for improvement that would better match their desire for conservative growth and income. After discussing several options, Bob and his wife chose the strategy that best fit their situation. Over the next 2 years, we reviewed on a regular basis, making adjustments as necessary. At our Annual Review in early 2011, Bob and his wife were very pleased with how well their accounts had done.

While some of their other friends had mentioned that they had made nothing in the year 2011, Bob said he and his wife just smiled contentedly knowing they were up thousands since becoming Clients. Their life was full of family, friends, travel, and enjoying being retired. Then things changed. Bob later told me that his wife had been saying she wasn't feeling right for a number of weeks. They thought it was just the flu or something.

When she didn't feel better, they went in to see their doctor. It was then they realized there was something serious. Shortly after Bob called me and shared the bad news. His wife of almost SO years had a rare disease, and it was terminal. After gathering myself from the initial shock, I did my best to comfort Bob, and told him to please feel free to call or come in to see me whenever he needed to. Over the next 12 months, I spoke to Bob in person or by phone 20 to 25 times, sometimes just a few minutes, but other times for an hour or so. Each time we spoke the news about his wife's condition grew worse. As her need for care increased, Bob consulted me for advice on where to draw the needed money from. Since I had dealt with this issue many times before, I was able to help him avoid the mistakes that cost many families thousands during these types of crisis times. Bob thanked me repeatedly.

Several weeks later I received a call from Bob saying Christmas would not be the same this year as his wife was not doing very well. I sent out a Christmas card and told Bob we would be praying for them. Shortly after the holidays I got a call from Bob that his wife had passed away. After doing my best to comfort him, I hung up the phone and felt compelled to write him a letter of encouragement. I also had my assistant send some flowers. When I saw the obituary, I immediately recognized there was a time issue. The Memorial Service was at the same time my wife had purchased tickets for us to take two of our granddaughters to a play at the Whiting. She had been planning this excursion for 3 months, and we were all looking forward to our "date". After talking with my wife, we mutually decided that I needed to go to the Memorial Service to be an encouragement to Bob. So after dropping off my wife and granddaughters at the Whiting, I went to the Memorial Service. The Fiddler on the Roof would have to fiddle without me. I did get back in time to see the closing act with my wife and granddaughters. We then capped off the afternoon with dinner together.

As I met Bob earlier this week, making sure we had taken care of every detail concerning his recent loss, Bob thanked me again for "being there for him". I could see in his eyes that he really meant it.

Later that night I called Bob to let him know answers to a couple tax questions he had. I also updated him on a life insurance claim from an old policy she had that he was having trouble with, that I had handled for him. Bob was shocked that I got back to him so soon. He thanked me again.

After I hung up the phone, I sat at my desk for a few minutes and thought about Bob and the events of the last 12 months. How I was able to be there for him, and how much it meant to him. I was thankful that I had made the decision <u>not</u> to be like so many of the other advisors, brokers, or agents I know in our area who boast of having 1000, or 3000, or 5000 clients "on the books". Because, if I did have several thousand "clients", how could I have been there for Bob? There just would not have been enough hours in my day to do it. So I am proud to say that I no longer try to run myself ragged trying to be all things to all people. That is an impossible task. And it is not fair to the client or to me. Nowadays I focus my time, expertise, and attention providing the same high level of personal concierge style service on my limited number of Platinum Member Clients, who, like Bob, understand and appreciate the benefits.

About the Authors

David Boike, ChFC
Host of NBC 25's "Money Matters"
Founder of Retirement Resources, LLC
Chartered Financial Consultant

Dave is a locally well-known financial educator, host of NBC 25's 'Money Matters' and author of "High Tide: A Practical Guide for Affluent Retirees to Protect, Profit and Prosper from the Coming Financial Storm." Dave's goal on 'Money Matters' is to discuss pertinent, current, and helpful financial information. For 32 years, Dave has been teaching investors how to preserve their assets, increase their income, and reduce income taxes.

Dave also serves as a Chartered Financial Consultant, a designation awarded only to experienced advisors who have completed a 10-course study program, through the American College in Pennsylvania, focusing on Tax, Investment, Risk Management, Retirement and Estate Planning. In addition, he is an approved member of the International Association of Registered Financial Planners, and the Society of Financial Service Professionals.

Dave is also a contributing author of '21st Century Wealth : an easy to read book for those already retired or those planning for a financially rewarding retirement. His insight and opinions are sought after by various media sources including The Wall Street journal, "Smart Money Magazine", Detroit Business Hour, TV 25, TV 12, and various radio stations. Dave was also recently featured in 'Senior Market Advisor' magazine for his outstanding service to the community.

For three years in a row, Dave has been named a 5 Star Wealth Manager, an award only given to the top 7% of advisors in each state. The 5 Star Wealth Manager status is only advisors who have a 95% or higher client satisfaction rating.

His Firm, Retirement Resources, LLC, has been recognized annually as one of the top Advisory firms in the country and has an A+ rating from the Better Business Bureau.

Recently Dave was featured on a new TV series created to educate Retirees on key issues named "The Consumer Advocate" which is out to air on many of the major networks in 2013. The information he shared will also appear in a new book co-authored with Best Selling Author Brian Tracy entitled "The Ultimate Success Guide," which is also due out
in early 2013.

Dave and his wife, Cherie, are the proud parents of 2 sons and 6 grandchildren. They are active members of a church, where he has served on the Deacon's board for over 15 years. In his free time, Dave enjoys playing basketball, going up north, reading, meeting new people, spending time with family and friends, and traveling.

DJ Boike, RFC
Host of NBC 25's "Money Matters"
Vice President of Retirement Resources, LLC
Investment Advisory Representative

DJ is a locally well-known financial educator and author of "High Tide: A Practical Guide for Affluent Retirees to Protect Profit and Prosper from the Coming Financial Storm." DJ's goal in "High Tide" is to discuss pertinent, current, and helpful financial information Retirees need to know. For over 10 years, DJ has been teaching investors how to preserve their assets, increase their income, and reduce income taxes.

DJ also serves as an Investment Advisory Representative a license awarded only to experienced advisors who have completed a series of tests administered by the State of Michigan, focusing on Tax, Investment, Risk Management, Retirement and Estate Planning. In addition, he is an approved member of the International Association of Registered Financial Planners.

"High Tide" is an easy to read book for those already retired or those planning for a financially rewarding retirement. His insight and opinions are sought after by various media sources including The Clarkston News, Tri County Times, TV 25, TV 12, and various radio stations. DJ was also featured in ' INC' magazine for his outstanding service to the community.

For three years in a row, Retirement Resources, LLC has been nam ed a 5 Star Wealth Manager, an award only given to the top 7% of advisors in each state. The 5 Star Wealth Manager status is only advisors who have a 95% or higher client satisfaction rating.

Retirement Resources, LLC has been recognized annually as one of the top Advisory firms in the country and has an A+ rating from the Better Business Bureau.

Recently DJ was featured on a new T.V. series created to educate Retirees on key issues named "The Consumer Advocate" which is out to air on many of the major networks in 2013. The information he shared will also appear in a new book co-authored with Best Selling Author Brian Tracy entitled "The Ultimate Success Guide," which is also due out in early 2013.

DJ has been married to his lovely wife, Jennifer, for 10 years. He is the proud father of 4 children, Gwyn, Ava, Boston, and Cooper. He is also a faithful member of Bethany Baptist Church.

19580142R00065

Made in the USA
Charleston, SC
01 June 2013